Fun
Bible
Q&A

Fun Bible Q&A

1,250 Challenging
Trivia Questions

BARBOUR
PUBLISHING

© 2006 by Barbour Publishing, Inc.

Compiled by JoAnne Simmons.

ISBN 978-1-61626-683-7

eBook Editions:
Adobe Digital Edition (.epub) 978-1-60742-760-5
Kindle and MobiPocket Edition (.prc) 978-1-60742-761-2

Content previously published in *The 365-Day Bible Trivia Challenge*.

Published by Barbour Publishing, P.O. Box 719, Uhrichsville, OH 44683, www.barbourbooks.com.

Our mission is to publish and distribute inspirational products offering exceptional value and biblical encouragement to the masses.

Member of the
Evangelical Christian
Publishers Association

Printed in the United States of America.

Introduction

What was Matthew's occupation before he became a disciple of Jesus?

What kind of animal helped Samson burn the grain fields of his enemies?
>   *a) lightning bugs*
>   *b) lions*
>   *c) donkeys*
>   *d) foxes*

True or False: Another name for Jesus' mother is Mary Magdalene.

Do not let the _____ _____ _____ while you are still angry (Ephesians 4:26 NIV).

Match: Vashti. . .
>   *a) another name for Esther*
>   *b) queen of Persia*
>   *c) Mordecai's cousin*

Test your scriptural knowledge with *Fun Bible Q & A*! Over the course of 250 quizzes—a total of 1,250 questions—you'll be challenged on your recall of the fascinating people and places, times and teachings, objects and oddities of the Bible. Can you answer them all correctly?

Inside this book, you'll be tested by multiple-choice questions, fill-in-the-blanks, open-ended queries, true or false statements, matching quizzes, and Connect the Thots stumpers. To "connect the thots," you'll need to determine the common theme among three seemingly unrelated ideas. For example, the connection among

- a worm-eaten plant
- an unusual fish
- a sinful city of 120,000

would be *the story of Jonah*. Answers for each day's questions are located at the bottom of each page—upside down, so you can't peek.

Ready to begin? Good—because the quizzes start on the next page. *Enjoy!*

1. What sound, according to the apostle Paul, causes every knee in heaven to bow?

2. What, in addition to *grace*, did the apostle John say Jesus, the Word, was "full of"?
   a) truth
   b) power
   c) love
   d) hope

3. True or False: Although Jesus was rejected in many cities, He was warmly received in His hometown of Nazareth.

4. What did Jesus do to serve His disciples at the Last Supper?

5. Connect the Thots:
   Egypt
   Capernaum
   Nazareth

Answers:

1. the name of Jesus (Philippians 2:10 NIV)
2. a (John 1:14 KJV)
3. False (Matthew 13:57)
4. He washed their feet (John 13:14)
5. places Jesus lived (Matthew 2:13–15; Matthew 4:12–13; Luke 4:14–16)

1. King Artaxerxes ordered that
    a) a festival be held each year to honor Jerusalem.
    b) everyone in Persia was to worship Jehovah.
    c) Jerusalem not be rebuilt until his command.
    d) no Jew was to work more than eight hours a day.

2. Which son of Jesse would succeed Saul as king?

3. Match: Vashti...
    a) another name for Esther
    b) queen of Persia
    c) Mordecai's cousin

4. Jonah told the Ninevites that they had how many days left before God would destroy them?

5. What Old Testament prophet was a shepherd from Tekoa?
    a) Micah
    b) Nahum
    c) Amos
    d) Zechariah

Quiz
2

1. What problem was the brave army commander Naaman healed of?
   a) blindness
   b) leprosy
   c) fever
   d) a hunched back

2. At what site did the Lord confound the language of the earth?

3. What angel announced the birth of Jesus to His mother, Mary?

4. Job's children were killed by
   a) Assyrians.
   b) fire.
   c) wind.
   d) hail.

5. What sea, according to the book of Hebrews, was crossed by the Israelites, by faith, "as by dry land"?

Quiz
3

1. When a Christian is too sad or upset to pray, what does the Holy Spirit do?

2. Complete the scripture:
   And as soon as we had heard these things, our hearts did melt, neither did there remain any more courage in any man, because of you: for the LORD your _____, he is _____ in heaven above, and in earth beneath.

3. According to the Lord's Prayer, where is God the Father?

4. Connect the Thots:
   immortal
   invisible
   the only wise

5. The disciples received the Holy Spirit during what special holiday?
   a) the Day of Atonement
   b) Pentecost
   c) Passover
   d) the Feast of Purim

Answers:

1. the Holy Spirit tells God what the Christian needs (Romans 8:26)
2. God, God (Joshua 2:11 kjv)
3. in heaven (Luke 11:2)
4. God (1 Timothy 1:17 kjv)
5. b (Acts 2:1-4)

1. How many letters did Paul write to the Corinthians?

2. Match: Aquila and Priscilla. . .
   a) sold idols in Ephesus.
   b) dealt in fine linen and wool.
   c) were tentmakers.

3. What were the Bereans famous for?

4. True or False: Eutychus was an old woman.

5. Complete the scripture:
   For she said within herself, If I may but _____ his garment, I shall be whole.

Answers:

1. two
2. c (Acts 18:2–3)
3. searching the scriptures (Acts 17:10–11)
4. False (Acts 20:9)
5. touch (Matthew 9:21 KJV)

1. Bethlehem is the city of _____.

2. The name of the place where the Thessalonians lived was
   a) Thesis.
   b) Thessalonica.
   c) Toronto.
   d) Thessa.

3. What river stopped flowing when priests carrying the ark reached the water's edge?

4. Connect the Thots:
   the Philippian jail
   Jesus' tomb
   Mt. Sinai

5. Match: Valley of Kidron. . .
   a) where Jesus gave the Beatitudes
   b) where Jesus brought Lazarus back from the dead
   c) near where Jesus was arrested

Answers:

5. c (John 18:1, 12 NIV)
4. sites of earthquakes (Acts 16:12–26; Matthew 28:1–6; Exodus 19:18)
3. Jordan (Joshua 3:15–16)
2. b
1. David (Luke 2:4)

Quiz
6

1. What are two of the four ways Luke says the young boy Jesus grew up?

2. What problem did Jesus heal two men of, saying, "According to your faith be it unto you"?
   a) leprosy
   b) blindness
   c) demon possession
   d) lameness

3. Connect the Thots:
   turn stones into bread
   jump from the top of the temple
   worship the devil

4. Jesus taught in stories. What are they called?

5. Complete the scripture:
   Come unto me, all ye that labour and are heavy laden, and I will give you _____.

Answers:

1. in wisdom, stature, favor with God, and favor with men (Luke 2:52)
2. b (Matthew 9:27–30 kjv)
3. the temptation of Christ (Matthew 4:1–11)
4. parables
5. rest (Matthew 11:28 kjv)

1. David was skillful at playing the
    a) electric organ.
    b) kazoo.
    c) accordion.
    d) harp.

2. What precious metal covered the ark and its carrying poles?

3. Connect the Thots:
    a mount
    groves
    Noah's dove

4. Match: Pillar of fire...
    a) covered the tabernacle at night
    b) at this sign, the Israelites set out on their journey
    c) at this sign, the Israelites made camp

5. When you glean a field, you
    a) sell it.
    b) gather leftover crops after the harvest.
    c) use it to bury the dead.
    d) cut down all the trees on it.

Answers:

1. d (1 Samuel 16:15–19)
2. gold (Exodus 25:10–14)
3. olives (Matthew 24:3; Joshua 24:13 NIV; Genesis 8:11)
4. a (Numbers 9:15–16)
5. b (Leviticus 19:9–10)

Quiz
8

• • • • • • • • • • • •

1. Connect the Thots:
   Jezebel
   Elymas
   a woman of Endor

2. Complete the scripture:
   Let not sin therefore _____ in your mortal body, that
   ye should obey it in the lusts thereof.

3. Match: Satan's destruction. . .
   a) by another flood
   b) by fire, before the thousand-year period of peace
   c) by fire, after the thousand-year period of peace

4. What disciple, watching Jesus' arrest and trial, claimed
   three times that he didn't know the Lord?

5. To reach heaven, the people tried to build
   a) the Empire State Building.
   b) a highway to heaven.
   c) the Tower of Babel.
   d) the Sears Building.

Answers:

5. c (Genesis 11:4, 8–9)
4. Peter (Matthew 26:69–75)
3. c (Revelation 20:7, 9–10)
2. reign (Romans 6:12 kjv)
1. witchcraft, or sorcery (2 Kings 9:22; Acts 13:8; 1 Samuel 28:7)

1. In what parable does Jesus quote, "My son. . .you are always with me, and everything I have is yours"?

2. Complete the scripture:
   Train up a child in the _____ he should go: and when he is old, he will not depart from it.

3. According to the book of Romans, "there is therefore now no" *what* "to them which are in Christ Jesus"?
   a) fear of death
   b) sorrow
   c) condemnation
   d) suffering

4. When the apostle Paul wrote that "to live is Christ," what did he say it is "to die"?

5. Connect the Thots:
   a net
   a pearl
   a mustard seed

Answers:

1. the Parable of the Lost, or Prodigal, Son (Luke 15 niv)
2. way (Proverbs 22:6 kjv)
3. c (Romans 8:1 kjv)
4. gain (Philippians 1:21 kjv)
5. objects in Jesus' parables (Matthew 13:47–50; Matthew 13:45–46; Matthew 13:31–32)

Quiz
10

• • • • • • • • • • •

1. What kind of bread were the Israelites to eat in their Passover celebration?

2. You can find the Ten Commandments in the following Old Testament book(s):
    a) Exodus
    b) Deuteronomy
    c) Exodus and Deuteronomy
    d) Genesis

3. Match: Gehazi...
    a) asked Naaman for two talents of silver.
    b) lied to Elisha and became leprous.
    c) asked Elijah for a cake of bread.

4. How many books are in the Bible?

5. The Romans were
    a) Jewish.
    b) Catholic.
    c) Gentiles.
    d) popular.

Answers:

5. c (Romans 11:13)
4. sixty-six
3. b (2 Kings 5:20–27)
2. c (Exodus 20:1-17; Deuteronomy 5:7–21)
1. unleavened (Numbers 9:10–11)

1. How old was the boy Jesus when He amazed people in the temple with His spiritual insights?

2. Connect the Thots:
   myrrh
   frankincense
   gold

3. When does scripture say that Jesus was chosen to come to earth and offer a sacrifice for our sins?

4. Match: How Jesus as Redeemer will return. . .
   a) Jesus will come again in the clouds.
   b) An earthquake will announce Jesus' second coming.
   c) Jesus will come amid loud claps of thunder and lightning.

5. When Jesus saw the moneychangers at the temple, He
   a) bought three doves and two goats.
   b) asked for change for the vending machines.
   c) asked what time the Bible study on the book of Revelation would occur.
   d) overturned their tables and angrily rebuked them.

Answers:

1. twelve (Luke 2:41–52)
2. gifts for the baby Jesus (Matthew 2:1–11)
3. before the creation of the world (1 Peter 1:18–20 NIV)
4. a (Luke 21:27–28)
5. d (John 2:13–16)

1. What third son did Eve say God gave her in place of the murdered Abel?

2. True or False: Jacob was renamed Israel.

3. Complete the scripture:
   Noah found _____ in the eyes of the LORD.

4. After Moses' death, who succeeded him?

5. We first meet Aaron in the Bible when he is
   a) a baby being hidden from Pharaoh.
   b) speaking to Pharaoh's daughter about a Hebrew
      nurse for Moses.
   c) writing down the Ten Commandments.
   d) appointed by God to help Moses.

Quiz
13

1. How many days did God use to create the world and everything in it?

2. True or False: John the Baptist begged Jesus for the privilege of baptizing Him since He is the Son of God.

3. Connect the Thots:
   the Shunammite's son
   Eutychus
   Lazarus

4. How many loaves of bread, along with two fish, did Jesus turn into a meal for five thousand men?

5. Match: Calming the storm...
   a) Jesus was piloting the boat.
   b) Jesus was having a meal.
   c) Jesus was sleeping.

1. What special talent did God give to Daniel that would later help the king?

2. God promises believers
   a) earthly riches.
   b) eternal life.
   c) manna.
   d) a year's supply of Rice a Roni, the San Francisco treat.

3. What form did the Holy Spirit take when He descended on Jesus after His baptism in the Jordan River?

4. Complete the scripture:
   Create in me a clean heart, O God; and renew a _____ spirit within me.

5. What three things did God create on the fourth day to light the universe?

Answers:

1. understanding of visions and dreams (Daniel 1:17)
2. b (John 3:16)
3. a dove (Matthew 3:13–17)
4. right (Psalm 51:10 kjv)
5. the sun, the moon, and the stars (Genesis 1:14–19)

1. What apostle and New Testament author was originally known as Saul?

2. True or False: John the Baptist wrote the Gospel of John.

3. What disciple betrayed Jesus with a kiss?

4. Connect the Thots:
   an apostle
   a tanner
   a sorcerer

5. Match: Deaths of the disciples...
   a) Peter drowned in the Sea of Galilee.
   b) James was martyred by King Herod.
   c) John was crucified upside down.

1. Where did God plant a garden and place the man, Adam, He had created?

2. Connect the Thots:
   Babel
   Siloam
   Jerusalem

3. What site did Abraham purchase as a family burial place?

4. King Artaxerxes found the city of Jerusalem to be
   a) peaceful.
   b) fun loving.
   c) on the cutting edge of technology.
   d) rebellious.

5. True or False: When the New Testament was written, Israel was the largest and most powerful nation on earth.

Answers:

1. Eden (Genesis 2:8)
2. places with towers (Genesis 11:5–9; Luke 13:4; 2 Chronicles 26:9)
3. the cave of Machpelah (Genesis 23:19)
4. d (Ezra 4:19)
5. False. Israel was no longer an independent nation but a province of a larger empire.

Quiz
17

1. What name, meaning "God with us," did Isaiah prophesy for Jesus?

2. Complete the scripture:
   [Jesus] bare our sins in his own body on the _____, that we, being dead to sins, should live unto righteousness.

3. Match: A sign Jesus is the Prince of Peace. . .
   a) A lamb without blemish was at Jesus' baptism.
   b) A dove alit on Jesus after His baptism.
   c) A rainbow appeared overhead after Jesus' baptism.

4. What did Jesus ask the woman at the well to give Him?

5. What important news did Jesus tell the woman at the well about Himself?

Answers:

1. Immanuel or Emmanuel (Isaiah 7:14; Matthew 1:22–23)
2. tree (1 Peter 2:24 kjv)
3. b (Matthew 3:16)
4. a drink of water (John 4:7)
5. that He is the Messiah (John 4:25–26)

1. Unleavened bread is made
   a) without yeast.
   b) with yeast.
   c) in an oven that is off balance.
   d) by the Wonder company.

2. What product were the Israelites, as slaves of Egypt, forced to make?

3. Connect the Thots:
   King Ahasuerus's scepter
   a calf-shaped idol
   the streets of the new Jerusalem

4. Match: Lentil stew. . .
   a) served in the Parable of the Lost Son
   b) served at the wedding in Cana
   c) what Jacob made Esau

5. True or False: The first bird Noah sent away from the ark was a dove.

Answers:

5. False (Genesis 8:7–8)
4. c (Genesis 25:34)
3. golden things (Esther 8:1–4; Exodus 32:2–4; Revelation 21:2, 21)
2. bricks (Exodus 5:4–8)
1. a (Exodus 12:20)

1. What relationship did Abram claim to his wife, Sarai, to try to gain favor with the Egyptians?

2. Connect the Thots:
   Cain
   Barabbas
   the devil

3. What overindulgers in food, according to the Proverbs, should be avoided?

4. If we say we have no sin, we are fooling
   a) ourselves.
   b) our parents.
   c) our teachers.
   d) our friends.

5. What did the Lord do when He saw that men were trying to build a tower to reach heaven?

Answers:

1. brother to sister (Genesis 12:10–20)

2. murderers (Genesis 4:8; Mark 15:7; John 8:44)

3. gluttons (Proverbs 23:20–21)

4. a (1 John 1:8)

5. He caused them to speak different languages and scattered them over the earth (Genesis 11:7–8).

1. What did Jesus command His followers to show to their enemies?

2. Complete the scripture:
Work out your own salvation with fear and _____.

3. On what surface did Jesus say a wise man built his house?

4. What type of relationship did Paul tell the Galatians their salvation gave them to God "through Christ"?
   a) friends
   b) heirs
   c) students
   d) subjects

5. Match: The kingdom of heaven. . .
   a) is like a ketchup seed.
   b) is like a lost sapphire.
   c) is like yeast in dough.

Answers:

1. love (Luke 6:35)
2. trembling (Philippians 2:12 kjv)
3. on rock (Matthew 7:24)
4. b (Galatians 4:7 kjv)
5. c (Matthew 13:33 niv)

1. An epistle is a
   a) letter.
   b) book.
   c) novel.
   d) wife of an apostle.

2. What physical condition of Elisha was once mocked by young people—leading to their mauling by bears?

3. Connect the Thots:
   Pentecost
   Jesus walks on water
   Job's children

4. Match: King Jehoash. . .
   a) was told by Elisha to strike the ground with his arrows.
   b) struck the ground five times with his arrows, upon Elisha's instruction.
   c) was told by Elijah to strike the ground three times.

5. When the psalmist David wrote, "Bless the LORD, O my soul," what three-word phrase did he remind himself to "forget not"?

Answers:

1. a
2. baldness (2 Kings 2:23–24)
3. strong winds (Acts 2:1–2; Matthew 14:26–32; Job 1:18–19)
4. a (2 Kings 13:14–18 NIV)
5. all his benefits (Psalm 103:2 KJV)

Quiz
22

● ● ● ● ● ● ● ● ● ● ●

1. How many days had Jesus fasted in the desert when Satan tempted Him to turn stones into bread?

2. What word completes Jesus' quote "Thy word is..."?
   a) wisdom
   b) power
   c) hope
   d) truth

3. Complete the scripture:
   Then said Jesus unto his disciples, If any man will come after me, let him _____ himself, and take up his cross, and follow me.

4. Match: Good Shepherd...
   a) Baby Jesus was greeted first by shepherds.
   b) Jesus was raised by Joseph, a shepherd.
   c) Many of Jesus' disciples were shepherds.

5. Who will judge all of us?

Answers:

1. forty (Matthew 4:1–4)
2. d (John 17:17 kjv)
3. deny (Matthew 16:24 kjv)
4. a (Luke 2:15–18)
5. Jesus Christ (Romans 14:10)

1. Gideon's story is found in which Bible book?
   a) Judges
   b) Matthew
   c) Exodus
   d) Nehemiah

2. What Old Testament prophet once had his name changed to "Belteshazzar"?

3. Connect the Thots:
   Samson
   Deborah
   Ehud

4. Who does James say "believed God, and it was imputed [or credited] unto him for righteousness"?
   a) Abraham
   b) Solomon
   c) Noah
   d) Joshua

5. What prostitute urged the men of Jericho to quickly pursue two Israelite spies—while she harbored those spies in her own home?

Answers:

5. Rahab (Joshua 2:1–6)

4. a (James 2:23 kjv)

3. judges, or "deliverers," of Israel (Judges 16:30–31 kjv; Judges 4:4 kjv; Judges 3:15)

2. Daniel (Daniel 1:7)

1. a (Judges 6:11–8:32)

1. What disaster caused Jacob to send his sons from Canaan to Egypt?

2. Connect the Thots:
   David spares King Saul's life
   Obadiah hides one hundred prophets of God
   Lazarus is raised to life

3. What significant event concerning man's lifespan occurred during Noah's time?

4. Match: Walking on water. . .
   a) The apostles thought Jesus was a ghost.
   b) Peter sank to the bottom of the lake.
   c) The apostles still did not believe Jesus was the Son of God.

5. What did God take from Adam to make Eve?

1. What did Jesus promise that God the Father would give to anyone who asked?

2. We can have peace with God through
   a) random acts of kindness.
   b) helping an old lady cross the street every day.
   c) making sure we give 10 percent of our allowance to church every Sunday.
   d) faith in our Lord Jesus Christ.

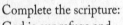

3. Complete the scripture:
   God is our refuge and _____, a very present help in trouble.

4. What did Hannah request of God?

5. How did God answer Hannah's prayer?

• • • • • • • • • • • •

1. What nickname did Jesus give to the disciple brothers James and John?

2. True or False: John was the first disciple called by Jesus.

3. Connect the Thots:
   John the Baptist
   James, brother of the apostle John
   Stephen

4. What was the first name of the apostle known as "the zealot" or "Zelotes"?

5. Match: Eunice...
   a) mother of John Mark
   b) mother of Barnabas
   c) mother of Timothy

1. What part of the body completes the meaning of the name Golgotha: "the place of the. . ."?

2. Connect the Thots:
    Nebo
    Ararat
    Sinai

3. Kerith Ravine was located
    a) east of Eden.
    b) west of the Jordan.
    c) east of Jordan.
    d) near one of Michael Jordan's homes.

4. When the Israelites moved into the Promised Land, what city became the permanent home of the tabernacle?

5. What town, whose name means "house of bread," was near the site where Rachel was buried?

• • • • • • • • • • • •

1. What did Jesus and Peter pay with a coin found in a fish's mouth?

2. Jesus called Himself
   a) the manna of man.
   b) divine.
   c) the bread of life.
   d) the world's best teacher.

3. Who ministered to Jesus after His temptation in the wilderness?

4. Match: High Priest. . .
   a) Jesus was descended from the high priest Nadab.
   b) Jesus was descended from the tribe of Levi.
   c) Jesus is a high priest of the order of Melchizedek.

5. What will happen to those who say that Jesus is the Son of God?

Answers:

1. tax (Matthew 17:24–27)
2. c (John 6:43–48)
3. angels (Matthew 4:1, 11)
4. c (Hebrews 6:20 NIV)
5. God will live in them, and they will live in God (1 John 4:15).

1. In the Bible, Christians are sometimes referred to as
    a) goats.
    b) vipers.
    c) serpents.
    d) sheep.

2. What two foods were said to flow in the land of
   Canaan?

3. Connect the Thots:
    grass
    a fig tree
    a man's hand

4. Match: Grapes. . .
    a) what Jael served to Sisera
    b) produce carried back from Canaan by Israel's spies
    c) what Ahab choked on

5. What two types of materials were used to make the
   curtains in the tabernacle?

Quiz
30

1. True or False: Ahab angered God more than any king of Israel before him.

2. What priests, the two sons of Eli, were judged for treating the Lord's offerings with contempt?

3. Jonah boarded a ship to Tarshish because
    a) Tarshish was on the way to Nineveh.
    b) he had been told to take a priest from Tarshish with him.
    c) he wanted to flee from the Lord.
    d) he needed a catch of fish to take along as food.

4. According to the three-part warning in the book of James, "when lust hath conceived, it bringeth forth sin: and sin, when it is finished, bringeth forth" *what*?

5. Eve was tempted by a
    a) serpent.
    b) ladybug.
    c) dinosaur.
    d) spider.

Answers:

5. a (Genesis 3:1)
4. death (James 1:15 kjv)
3. c (Jonah 1:3)
2. Hophni and Phinehas (1 Samuel 1:3; 2:12–17)
1. True (1 Kings 16:30–33)

Quiz
31

1. Complete the scripture:
   In the beginning was the _____, and the _____ was with God, and the _____ was God.

2. What tiny seed did Jesus liken the kingdom of heaven to?

3. John said Jesus would baptize with the Holy Ghost and with
   a) wine.
   b) fire.
   c) ashes.
   d) water.

4. What phrase completes the apostle Paul's quotation about suffering for Christ's sake: "For when I am weak..."?

5. Connect the Thots:
   honor your father and mother
   don't murder
   don't covet

Answers:

5. the Ten Commandments (Exodus 20:1–17)
4. then am I strong (2 Corinthians 12:10 kjv)
3. b (Matthew 3:1, 11)
2. mustard (Matthew 13:1–3, 31–32)
1. Word, Word, Word (John 1:1 kjv)

1. What substance appeared on Gideon's fleece one night—but not the next—to convince him he was working in God's will?

2. Match: Hazael. . .
    a) was told by Elisha that he would die.
    b) was told by Elisha that he would be king of Judah.
    c) asked Elisha if the king of Aram would get well.

3. True or False: Although Rahab's story is recorded in the Old Testament, she is mentioned at least twice in the New Testament.

4. Connect the Thots:
    the father of lies
    the accuser of the brethren
    Beelzebub

5. Who wrote the Epistle to the Hebrews?

Answers:

1. dew (Judges 6:36–40)
2. c (2 Kings 8:9)
3. True (Hebrews 11:31; James 2:25)
4. names of Satan (John 8:44; Revelation 12:9–10 kjv; Matthew 12:24)
5. We do not know, although some Bible scholars think Paul the apostle wrote it.

1. Match: Jesus...
    a) upon birth, wrapped in purple cloth by Mary
    b) upon birth, encompassed in Joseph's robes
    c) upon birth, wrapped in bands of cloth by Mary

2. What did a Simon from Cyrene carry for Jesus as He walked to His execution?

3. Complete the scripture:
   Whosoever drinketh of the water that I shall give him shall never _____.

4. Some people said Jesus was
    a) Elijah.
    b) John the Baptist.
    c) Jeremiah.
    d) all of the above.

5. True or False: Jesus approved of the process of buying and selling sacrificial doves and other animals in the temple, since it was so convenient for everyone concerned.

Answers:

1. c (Luke 2:7)
2. His cross (Luke 23:26)
3. thirst (John 4:14 kjv)
4. d (Matthew 16:13–14)
5. False (Mark 11:15)

1. Which tribe of Israel had responsibility for moving the ark?

2. Rahab hid the spies
    a) on the roof of her house.
    b) at the house of a friend.
    c) in the cellar of her house.
    d) with a priest at the temple.

3. Leah's story is recorded in what book of the Bible?

4. Connect the Thots:
    Esther
    Jezebel
    Athaliah

5. Match: Jehoiakim...
    a) king who fled from the Babylonians against Jeremiah's advice
    b) king of Babylon
    c) king who burned Jeremiah's scrolls

Answers:

5. c (Jeremiah 36:1, 23, 27)
4. queens (Esther 2:17; 1 Kings 16:29–31; 2 Chronicles 22:10–12)
3. Genesis
2. a (Joshua 2:3–6)
1. Levi (Deuteronomy 10:8)

1. What special celebration saw property that had been sold returned to its original owners?

2. Connect the Thots:
   spying in Canaan
   the sun stands still
   Jericho's walls fall

3. Match: Healing a paralyzed man. . .
   a) The man was brought in through a window.
   b) Jesus healed him without seeing him.
   c) The man was lowered through the roof.

4. How many smooth stones did David pick up to fight Goliath?

5. What did the Philistines do after David killed Goliath?

Quiz
36

1. What did God tell Moses he was standing on when he approached the burning bush?

2. Complete the scripture:
   O my God, I trust in thee: let me not be _____, let not mine enemies triumph over me.

3. How many times did God call Samuel before Samuel answered, "Speak; for thy servant heareth"?

4. When God spoke to Samuel, Samuel thought he was being called by
   a) Eli.
   b) Hannah.
   c) an angel.
   d) the alien E.T.

5. The Lord told Samuel He planned to
   a) bless Eli.
   b) bless Eli's sons.
   c) allow Eli to win a dream house in a raffle.
   d) punish Eli's house because Eli's sons were evil.

Answers:

5. d (1 Samuel 3:11–14)
4. a (1 Samuel 3:5)
3. Samuel answered the Lord on the fourth call (1 Samuel 3:8–10 kjv).
2. ashamed (Psalm 25:2 kjv)
1. holy ground (Exodus 3:3–5)

1. What Caesar ordered the census that brought Mary, expecting the baby Jesus, to Bethlehem?

2. What early Christian leader explained the way of salvation to an Ethiopian eunuch, who accepted Christ, was baptized, and "went on his way rejoicing"?
   a) Philip
   b) Andrew
   c) Nathanael
   d) Apollos

3. What physical characteristic initially hindered Zacchaeus from seeing Jesus?

4. Connect the Thots:
   missionary companion of the apostle Paul
   correspondent with Theophilus
   beloved physician

5. True or False: Paul was in prison when he wrote to Philemon.

1. What mountain, where Moses received the Ten Commandments, shook as the Lord came down on it?

2. Connect the Thots:
   Pharpar
   Pison
   Jordan

3. In what city did silversmiths—fearing the effect of Paul's preaching on their idol-making business—stir up a riot?

4. Match: Tyre...
   a) where Peter restored Tabitha to life
   b) where Jesus restored a widow's son to life
   c) where Jesus healed a demon-possessed girl

5. Where will the ark of the covenant ultimately be found?

1. What town in Galilee was the boyhood home of Jesus?

2. Match: Jesus...
   a) After His crucifixion, His clothes were given back to Mary.
   b) Peter asked the soldiers for Jesus' clothes.
   c) He wore a seamless undergarment.

3. True or False: Joseph and Mary reared Jesus as a Christian.

4. Who asked Jesus to perform his first miracle?
   a) Joseph
   b) Mary
   c) Elijah
   d) a nervous bridegroom

5. True or False: Since it was important that Jesus not damage His reputation as God's Son, he avoided associating with outcasts and sinners while here on earth.

1. Noah sent a dove out of the ark
    a) to see if the waters had gone down so they could leave the ark.
    b) to find Dove Bars because they were hungry.
    c) to dig up some worms for the other birds on the ark.
    d) to symbolize peace in the world.

2. What did the fearful Israelite spies who explored Canaan say they looked like compared to the giants they saw there?

3. Connect the Thots:
    shekel
    talent
    pound

4. Match: Fish. . .
    a) what Jesus served some disciples for breakfast
    b) created on the fourth day
    c) created on the third day

5. True or False: Noah waited seven days between each time he sent the dove out from the ark.

Answers:

5. True (Genesis 8:10, 12)
4. a (John 21:4–13)
3. measurements of weight (Genesis 24:22; 2 Samuel 12:30; John 19:39)
2. grasshoppers (Numbers 13:17, 33)
1. a (Genesis 8:1, 8)

1. What did the apostle Paul say "dwelleth in me" and caused him to struggle spiritually?
   a) evil
   b) carnality
   c) falsehood
   d) sin

2. What husband and wife died after lying about the amount of money they gave as an offering?

3. If Eve would eat the forbidden fruit, the serpent promised her
   a) clothing.
   b) riches.
   c) a starring role in a movie.
   d) knowledge of good and evil.

4. Why did God reject Saul as king?

5. What unaccepted offering provoked Cain's murder of Abel?

1. What did Jesus say was more likely to go through the eye of a needle than for a rich man to enter heaven?

2. What follows "In all thy ways acknowledge him" in a beloved passage of Proverbs?
   a) and he shall direct thy paths.
   b) and he shall sustain thee.
   c) and he shall hear thy prayers.
   d) and he shall vindicate thee.

3. Instead of suing your enemy and taking him to court, what course of action did Jesus advise?

4. Complete the scripture:
   For by grace are ye saved through _____; and that not of yourselves: it is the gift of God.

5. Match: The Lost Son. . .
   a) The father gave his lost son a ring and sandals.
   b) The father gave his lost son a chariot and horses.
   c) The father gave his lost son a vineyard.

Answers:

5. a (Luke 15:21–22)
4. faith (Ephesians 2:8 kjv)
3. settling matters out of court (Matthew 5:25)
2. a (Proverbs 3:6 kjv)
1. a camel (Matthew 19:23–24)

1. What does the "lover" in the Song of Solomon twice compare his "beloved's" hair to?

2. A Pharisee was a
   a) civil servant.
   b) university teacher.
   c) doctor of the law.
   d) tax collector.

3. What did Jacob wear to make his father, whose eyes were dim with age, think he was hairy like Esau?

4. Connect the Thots:
   Jesus' disciples
   tribes of Israel
   gates of the new Jerusalem

5. Name at least two people of faith described in Hebrews.

Answers:

1. a flock of goats (Song of Solomon 4:1; 6:5)
2. c (Acts 5:34 KJV)
3. the skins of goat kids (Genesis 27:15–16)
4. twelve (Matthew 10:1; Genesis 49:28; Revelation 21:2, 21)
5. Abel, Enoch, Noah, Abraham, Sarah, Isaac, Jacob, Joseph, the parents of Moses, Moses, Rahab (Hebrews 11)

Quiz
44

• • • • • • • • • • •

1. What "Mount of" was frequented by Jesus?

2. Match: Jesus. . .
    a) fasted before being baptized by John the Baptist.
    b) fasted before choosing His disciples.
    c) fasted before meeting Satan.

3. Who saw Satan fall as lightning from heaven?

4. What color horse does Jesus ride during the great battle in the book of Revelation?
    a) gold
    b) red
    c) white
    d) black

5. What door-openers to the kingdom of heaven did Jesus say He would give to Peter?

1. What evil woman led Israel's King Ahab, her husband, into Baal worship?

2. What king of Judah "trusted in the Lord God of Israel"—and was rewarded with an extra fifteen years of life?
   a) Hezekiah
   b) Manasseh
   c) Asa
   d) Jehoshaphat

3. What job did the youthful David have before his anointing as king?

4. Connect the Thots:
   a dove
   a rainbow
   the mountains of Ararat

5. Match: Jotham...
   a) proclaimed himself king of Shechem.
   b) was the only brother to escape Abimelech's wrath.
   c) was the last judge of Israel.

Answers:

5. b (Judges 9:4–5)
4. the story of Noah and the ark (Genesis 8:8–9; Genesis 9:16–17; Genesis 8:1–4)
3. shepherd (1 Samuel 16:11–13)
2. a (2 Kings 18:1–5, 20:1–6 kjv)
1. Jezebel (1 Kings 16:29–31)

Quiz
46

• • • • • • • • • • •

1. What illegal activity resulted in Daniel being thrown into the lions' den?

2. Connect the Thots:
   at Cana in Galilee
   of the Lamb
   Jesus' parable of a king and his son

3. Match: Fiery furnace. . .
   a) Shadrach, Meshach, and Abednego wore only trousers in the furnace.
   b) King Nebuchadnezzar ordered the furnace seven times hotter.
   c) King Nebuchadnezzar saw five men inside the furnace.

4. Esther. . .
   a) held a triathlon to see who would be her king.
   b) won a beauty contest and married the king.
   c) paid the king a lot of money to marry her because she was ugly.
   d) was not Jewish.

5. From which tribe was King Saul?

Answers:

5. the tribe of Benjamin (1 Samuel 9:16)

4. b (Esther 2:5–17)

3. b (Daniel 3:19)

2. weddings (John 2:1; Revelation 19:7; Matthew 22:1–2)

1. praying to God (Daniel 6:6–14)

Quiz
47

1. What storm-related phenomenon is likened to God's voice in the books of Job and John?

2. The Lord told Samuel to
    a) let the people see how a king would rule.
    b) sacrifice two goats and a perfect male ram.
    c) produce two more sons worthier to be judges.
    d) store grain for seven years because there would be seven years of famine.

3. When the people asked for a king, whom did the Lord say they were really rejecting?

4. When we pray, whose plan shall be carried out?
    a) ours
    b) God's
    c) our pastor's
    d) our parents'

5. Who is in charge of seeking revenge for evil?

Answers:

5. God (Romans 12:19)
4. b (Romans 8:27)
3. the Lord Himself (1 Samuel 8:7)
2. a (1 Samuel 8:9)
1. thunder (Job 37:4–5; John 12:23–29)

1. What man, with a name like a Roman god, became a powerful preacher of Christ in the early church?

2. The Pharisees believed in
   a) life after death and the supernatural.
   b) life after death but not angels.
   c) neither life after death nor the supernatural.
   d) angels, but not in life after death.

3. What disciple found himself "weightless" enough to walk on water with Jesus—only as long as he kept his focus on the Lord?

4. Connect the Thots:
   locusts
   camel's hair
   wild honey

5. True or False: Mary Magdalene is mentioned in all four Gospels.

Answers:

5. True (Matthew 27:56; Mark 15:40; Luke 8:2; John 19:25)
4. John the Baptist (Matthew 3:1, 4)
3. Peter (Matthew 14:28–31)
2. a (Acts 23:6–9)
1. Apollos (Acts 18:24–26)

1. Where did God tell Isaac's father to sacrifice the young man as a burnt offering?

2. In what city did Silas and Paul—the former persecutor Saul—lead the local jailer to life in Christ?
   a) Troas
   b) Berea
   c) Philippi
   d) Athens

3. How many days would it take a person to walk through the city of Nineveh?

4. Match: Valley of Ben Hinnom...
   a) also known as Valley of Hope
   b) also known as Topheth
   c) also known as Valley of Despair

5. When the Israelites camped in the wilderness, on what side of the tabernacle did the tribes of Judah, Zebulun, and Issachar camp together?

Answers:

1. Moriah (Genesis 22:1–2)
2. c (Acts 16:19–34)
3. three (Jonah 3:3)
4. b (Jeremiah 19:6 NIV)
5. east (Numbers 2:1–9)

1. What, according to the prophet Isaiah, would Jesus carry on His shoulders?

2. Match: Jesus...
   a) said to fast as the Pharisees did.
   b) said to put oil on your head and wash your face.
   c) said not to fast.

3. When the Pharisees brought a woman to Jesus who was caught committing adultery, what did Jesus do first?

4. True or False: When Jesus drove demons from people, the demons proclaimed that Jesus was God's Son.

5. What did Jesus tell church members in Laodicea He would do with them if they opened the door to His knocking?

Answers:

5. eat with them (Revelation 3:14, 20)
4. True (Luke 4:41)
3. He bent down and started writing on the ground with His finger (John 8:4–6).
2. b (Matthew 5:1; 6:17)
1. the government (Isaiah 9:6)

1. What did the angels who visited Sodom do with Lot?

2. What vegetable did the complaining Israelites recall from their years of slavery in Egypt?

3. Connect the Thots:
   when Rebekah met Isaac
   straining out gnats
   the eye of a needle

4. Match: Vegetables. . .
   a) Daniel's diet for ten days
   b) Esther's beauty secret
   c) what Ruth picked in Boaz's fields

5. What animal saw the angel of the Lord?

1. What color is used to describe sin in the book of Isaiah?

2. According to Jesus, what was Satan "from the beginning"?
   a) a deceiver
   b) a rebel
   c) an enemy
   d) a murderer

3. What was the method of execution for a man who blasphemed the Lord's name with a curse?

4. True or False: God said Israel will be punished for her sins.

5. After they had sinned, what did Adam and Eve do when they heard God calling?

Answers:

5. They hid themselves (Genesis 3:8).
4. True (Hosea 8:1–14)
3. stoning (Leviticus 24:10–23)
2. d (John 8:44)
1. crimson or scarlet (Isaiah 1:18)

1. What did Paul tell Timothy that Christians should lift up in prayer?

2. What did the apostle Paul say he had learned, "in whatsoever state I am"?
   a) to be content
   b) always to pray
   c) God is good
   d) faith is sufficient

3. True or False: Paul always described himself in his letters as head of the church.

4. Complete the scripture:
   Let us therefore come boldly unto the _____ of grace, that we may obtain mercy, and find grace to help in time of need.

5. Match: The rich fool. . .
   a) The rich fool wanted to tear down his barns.
   b) A famine had destroyed the rich fool's crops.
   c) The rich fool lived to be 108 years old.

Answers:

5. a (Luke 12:16–20)

4. throne (Hebrews 4:16 kjv)

(Romans 1:1; Titus 1:1).

3. False. He referred to himself as a servant of Christ/servant of God

2. a (Philippians 4:11 kjv)

1. holy hands (1 Timothy 2:8)

1. Who wrote the Epistle of Jude?

2. What did John call the new Jerusalem he saw in a vision, coming down out of heaven?

3. God instructed Noah to make the ark
   a) 300 cubits long, 50 cubits wide, and 30 cubits high.
   b) 400 cubits long, 50 cubits wide, and 60 cubits high.
   c) 300 cubits long, 50 cubits wide, and 60 cubits high.
   d) 400 cubits long, 30 cubits wide, and 30 cubits high.

4. Connect the Thots:
   Joseph
   the ancient Israelites
   Onesimus

5. How many books are in the Old Testament?

Answers:

5. thirty-nine
4. slaves (Genesis 39:1–3; Exodus 2:23; Philemon 10–16)
3. a (Genesis 6:15)
2. the Holy City (Revelation 21:1–2)
1. Jude

1. Who did Jesus say He was calling to repentance when Pharisees asked why He ate with disreputable people?

2. What word described the crowd's response when Jesus used His authority to drive out evil spirits?

3. Match: Jesus...
    a) buried in a tomb with the patriarchs
    b) buried in Bethlehem
    c) buried in a garden tomb near the site of His crucifixion

4. What short word, meaning "trouble," did Jesus pronounce on the Pharisees seven times in one speech?

5. What did Jesus say a man could forfeit, negating the gain of "the whole world"?

1. What prophet of God challenged 450 prophets of Baal to see whose god would answer by fire?

2. What prophet resisted the temptation to accept money for healing the leper Naaman—then condemned his own servant to leprosy for taking Naaman's money dishonestly?
   a) Samuel
   b) Elijah
   c) Elisha
   d) Obadiah

3. What was Ruth doing the first time she saw Boaz, the man she would marry?

4. True or False: King Ahab was a wise ruler who worshiped Jehovah.

5. Connect the Thots:
   a favored son
   a dream of supremacy
   a coat of many colors

Answers:

5. Joseph (Genesis 37:3; Genesis 37:5–7; Genesis 37:3)
4. False (1 Kings 16:29–33)
3. gleaning (Ruth 2:2–8)
2. c (2 Kings 5:1–27)
1. Elijah (1 Kings 18:22–24)

1. What collapsed and killed eighteen people in a "news event" that Jesus used to encourage repentance?

2. After the flood, the Bible says that Noah
    a) planted a vegetable garden.
    b) planted a vineyard.
    c) bred goats and sheep.
    d) divided the land equally between his three sons.

3. Connect the Thots:
    the creation
    the fall of man
    the calling of Abraham

4. Match: Water from the rock. . .
    a) Aaron struck the rock at Horeb.
    b) Moses called the place "Meribah" because the people were happy.
    c) Moses struck the rock at Horeb.

5. True or False: The Feast of Unleavened Bread was established by God.

Answers:

1. a tower (Luke 13:2–5)
2. b (Genesis 8:15–18; 9:20)
3. events in the book of Genesis (Genesis 1–2:4; Genesis 3:17–19; Genesis 12:1–3)
4. c (Exodus 17:3–6)
5. True (Exodus 12:1, 17)

Quiz
58

● ● ● ● ● ● ● ● ● ● ● ●

1. Who is the Counselor whom Jesus says He will ask the Father to give His followers?

2. The book of Job relates how
   a) to get a good job.
   b) God protects and rewards those who love Him.
   c) to cover up those ugly sores.
   d) friends help out when the going gets tough.

3. What does God think of good works done in His name?

4. True or False: We can pray to God anytime.

5. When we pray to God, we should first
   a) praise Him.
   b) ask for whatever we want.
   c) ask for good weather.
   d) tell Him we haven't done anything wrong.

Answers:

5. a (Luke 11:2)
4. True. God listens to us any time of the day or night (Luke 18: 1-8).
3. He will not forget them (Hebrews 6:10).
2. b (Job 42:12-17)
1. the Holy Spirit (John 14:16-17)

Quiz
59

1. John says he wrote his book so you will
    a) feed the poor.
    b) be healthy, wealthy, and wise.
    c) be a good person.
    d) believe in Jesus Christ, the Son of God, and have
       life in His name.

2. What "prickly" physical ailment did Paul write about to the
   church at Corinth?

3. Felix was governor of
    a) Judea.
    b) Caesarea.
    c) Jerusalem.
    d) Rome.

4. Match: Ephraim. . .
    a) younger son of Joseph
    b) forefather of Jesus
    c) firstborn son of Joseph

5. King Herod sought the baby Jesus to
    a) worship Him.
    b) give Him gold, frankincense, and myrrh.
    c) give Mary and Joseph money for a hotel room.
    d) kill Him.

Answers:

1. d (John 20:31)
2. a thorn in the flesh (2 Corinthians 12:7)
3. b (Acts 23:23–24)
4. a (Genesis 48:8–20)
5. d (Matthew 2:13)

1. What city's walls fell at the shout of Joshua's army?

2. Rahab's house was located
   a) on a mountaintop.
   b) on the town wall.
   c) near a grape arbor
   d) just behind the entrance to the city.

3. What mount approximately five miles from Nazareth is reputed to be the traditional site of the Transfiguration?

4. Match: Beersheba...
   a) where Naaman was healed of leprosy
   b) where Samuel was raised in the temple
   c) where Elijah fled to escape Jezebel

5. What tribes of Israel settled east of the Jordan River?

Answers:

1. Jericho (Joshua 6:2–5, 20)
2. b (Joshua 2:3, 15)
3. Mount Tabor
4. c (1 Kings 19:1–3)
5. Gad, Reuben, and Manasseh (Joshua 18:7)

1. What Greek letter did Jesus pair with "Alpha" to describe Himself?

2. Match: Jesus...
   a) buried by Roman soldiers with guidance from the disciples
   b) buried by Joseph and Nicodemus
   c) buried by Mary and Mary Magdalene

3. What two commands on prayer, besides "knock," did Jesus give during His Sermon on the Mount?

4. Complete the verse:
   Heaven and earth shall _____ _____: but my words shall not _____ _____.

5. When Jesus said, "No man cometh unto the Father, but by me," what two names did He give Himself besides "the life"?

Quiz
62

1. What insects are mentioned by the writer of the book of James as destroyers of clothing?

2. Connect the Thots:
   the wise men and Jesus
   Wormwood
   the fourth day of creation

3. Match: Nehemiah. . .
   a) was a scribe for Cyrus in Jerusalem.
   b) kept the ark of the covenant in Jerusalem for David.
   c) rebuilt Jerusalem's walls after captivity.

4. What kind of tree supplied the wood for Aaron's rod that budded?

5. What metals did Tubal-cain work with?

1. How did Jesus instruct Judas Iscariot to do his evil work of betrayal?

2. When he was caught disobeying God, Adam blamed
   a) the serpent.
   b) bad programs on television.
   c) Cain.
   d) Eve.

3. Who convinced a prophet to sin by claiming he had a message from the angel of the Lord?

4. When he heard what Gehazi had done, Elisha
   a) rewarded him with half the money.
   b) complimented Gehazi on how smart he was.
   c) gave him a bigger Christmas bonus than usual for his efforts.
   d) said that Gehazi and his family would always be plagued with leprosy.

5. What two sons of Aaron were burned to death for offering unauthorized fire to the Lord?

Answers:

5. Nadab and Abihu (Leviticus 10:1–2)
4. d (2 Kings 5:25–27)
3. an old prophet who lived in Bethel (1 Kings 13:1–22)
2. d (Genesis 3:12)
1. quickly (John 13:26–27)

• • • • • • • • • • •

1. A good woman is
    a) virtuous.
    b) beautiful.
    c) rich.
    d) skinny.

2. What group of people, whom the disciples tried to keep from Jesus, did Jesus say are true possessors of the kingdom of heaven?

3. Complete the scripture:
   God resisteth the proud, but giveth grace unto the _____.

4. What, according to Peter, should Christians "be ready always to give" regarding "a reason of the hope that is in you"?

5. Match: The vineyard workers. . .
    a) The last vineyard workers were hired at the eleventh hour.
    b) The vineyard workers hired first received two denarii.
    c) The first vineyard workers were hired at the sixth hour.

Answers:

5. a (Matthew 20:1–9)
4. an answer (1 Peter 3:15 kjv)
3. humble (James 4:6 kjv)
2. little children (Matthew 19:14)
1. a (Proverbs 31:10 kjv)

1. What "skill" did a young slave girl lose when Paul cast a demon from her?

2. Connect the Thots:
   Saul and Abner
   Mordecai and Esther
   Mary and Elizabeth

3. What kind of stone, according to the apostle Paul, did God lay in Zion?

4. Match: One hundred fifty-three. . .
   a) prophets of Baal who opposed Elijah
   b) number of fish once caught by seven disciples
   c) age of Sarah when she died

5. What did Boaz buy on behalf of Naomi and Ruth?

1. What did Jesus write in the sand when a woman was brought before Him and accused of adultery?

2. Match: Jesus. . .
   a) wept over the future destruction of Jerusalem.
   b) wept when he saw John the Baptist.
   c) is never recorded as weeping in the Bible.

3. What repetitive phrase, according to Jesus, will not guarantee entry into the kingdom of heaven?

4. What Old Testament prophet's writing did Jesus read aloud in the Nazareth synagogue, telling the people, "This day is this scripture fulfilled in your ears"?
   a) Ezekiel
   b) Esaias, or Isaiah
   c) Hosea
   d) Jeremy, or Jeremiah

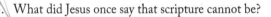

5. What did Jesus once say that scripture cannot be?

Answers:

5. broken (John 10:34–35)

4. b (Luke 4:16–21)

3. Lord, Lord (Matthew 7:21)

2. a (Luke 19:28, 39–44)

1. The Bible doesn't tell us what He wrote (John 8:6).

1. What "wild donkey of a man's" birth was foretold to his mother, Hagar?

2. Hannah's story takes place in
    a) 2 Samuel.
    b) 1 Chronicles.
    c) 1 Samuel.
    d) 2 Chronicles.

3. What miracle son was Abraham willing to sacrifice, "accounting that God was able to raise him up, even from the dead"?

4. Connect the Thots:
    lost donkeys
    a tall man
    anointing oil

5. Match: Baruch. . .
    a) wrote Jeremiah's words on a scroll.
    b) with Deborah, was a judge of Israel.
    c) accompanied Paul on his first missionary journey.

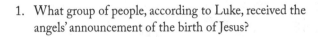

1. What group of people, according to Luke, received the angels' announcement of the birth of Jesus?

2. Match: Floating axhead. . .
   a) To retrieve it, Elisha threw a stick in the Jordan.
   b) To retrieve it, Gehazi jumped into the Jordan and drowned.
   c) To retrieve it, Elijah threw his cloak in the water.

3. What miracle did Peter perform in Joppa that spread Jesus' name in that city?

4. The Feast of Unleavened Bread was celebrated to remember
   a) not to run out of yeast.
   b) that man does not live by bread alone.
   c) how God brought the Israelites out of Egypt.
   d) that Jesus is the Messiah.

5. True or False: The Feast of Harvest celebrated the firstfruits of the harvest, and the Feast of Ingathering was celebrated at the end of the year.

Answers:

5. True (Exodus 23:16)
4. c (Exodus 12:17)
3. He raised Dorcas, also known as Tabitha, from the dead (Acts 9:36–40).
2. a (2 Kings 6:5–6)
1. shepherds (Luke 2:8–15)

1. Complete the scripture:
   God is a _____: and they that worship him must worship him in spirit and in truth.

2. The Lord told Samuel that people see outward beauty, but He sees their
   a) intelligence.
   b) possessions.
   c) time put in at Bible study class.
   d) hearts.

3. Who is the giver of wisdom?

4. To please God, a Christian must have
   a) given up chocolate for Lent.
   b) a long list of good deeds.
   c) self-denial.
   d) faith.

5. How does John define God?

1. What man, for whom a New Testament book is named, traveled to Corinth to help pick up an offering for needy saints?

2. Paul was sent to Felix by
   a) Claudius Lysias, a Roman soldier.
   b) King Agrippa.
   c) Caesar.
   d) Porcius Festus, Roman governor of Antioch.

3. What elderly prophetess met Mary, Joseph, and the baby Jesus at the temple and thanked God for the redemption to come?

4. Match: Dorcas. . .
   a) dealer in purple cloth
   b) known for her handmade robes
   c) made robes for Peter

5. Who wrote the Epistle to the Romans?

Answers:

5. Paul the Apostle
4. b (Acts 9:39)
3. Anna (Luke 2:27, 36–38)
2. a (Acts 23:24–26)
1. Titus (2 Corinthians 8:16–19)

1. What field was purchased by the chief priests with the "blood money" they got back from a remorseful Judas Iscariot?

2. Connect the Thots:
   liars and evil beasts
   the harbor of Phenice (Phoenix)
   Titus's parish

3. Match: Ramah...
   a) where Elisha trapped blinded Arameans
   b) where Samuel was born
   c) where Elijah went up to heaven in a whirlwind

4. Who was Isaac's favorite son?

5. As the book of Acts concludes, where in Rome is the apostle Paul?
   a) Caesar's palace
   b) a dungeon
   c) the Forum
   d) a rented house

• • • • • • • • •

1. What did Jesus say He would arrive in when He returns to earth "with power and great glory"?

2. What phrase, according to Matthew's Gospel, did Jesus repeat three times while battling Satan's temptation in the wilderness?
   a) Thou shalt not
   b) Get thee behind me
   c) Woe unto ye
   d) It is written

3. How many people lived in Nineveh in Jonah's time?

4. Match: Jesus. . .
   a) stood on the highest point of the temple in Jerusalem.
   b) refused Satan's offer to stand on the highest point of the temple in Jerusalem.
   c) chose His disciples outside the temple in Jerusalem.

5. How did Jesus say He came to provide life for His sheep?

Answers:

5. more abundantly, or to the full (John 10:7–10)
4. a (Luke 4:8–9)
3. more than 120,000 (Jonah 4:11 niv)
2. d (Matthew 4:3–10 kjv)
1. a cloud (Luke 21:27)

1. What was the composition of the feet of an enormous statue in King Nebuchadnezzar's dream—explained by Daniel?

2. Connect the Thots:
   two mites
   two pigeons
   five loaves and two fish

3. What creature of the wilderness does Malachi describe as laying waste to Esau's heritage?

4. Match: Figs. . .
   a) what Naboth grew in his orchard
   b) what God showed Jeremiah in two baskets
   c) what Eve gave to Adam

5. What job was given to cherubim after the expulsion of Adam and Eve from Eden?

• • • • • • • • • • •

1. Who paid Judas Iscariot to betray Jesus?

2. After Adam and Eve ate the forbidden fruit, God
     a) sent them out of Eden.
     b) let them stay in Eden.
     c) poured manna from heaven.
     d) told them to build an ark so he could begin the
        human race again.

3. What was cursed by God because of Adam?

4. Egypt and Edom will be punished for attacking
     a) the United States.
     b) Saudi Arabia.
     c) Jordan.
     d) Judah.

5. Who is the angel of the bottomless pit, whose name
   means "the destroyer," in the book of Revelation?

1. According to the book of Romans, how did God prove His love for sinners?
   a) Noah's rainbow
   b) Christ's death
   c) Paul's conversion
   d) John's Revelation

2. What two groups, according to Jesus in the Beatitudes, would inherit the kingdom of heaven?

3. Complete the scripture:
   We walk by faith, not by _____.

4. On what surface did Jesus say a foolish man built his house?

5. Match: The King's Ten Servants. . .
   a) The servant who earned five more minas took charge of five vineyards.
   b) The servant who earned ten more minas took charge of ten cities.
   c) The king's subjects went into mourning when the king left.

Answers:

1. b (Romans 5:8)
2. the poor in spirit, those persecuted for righteousness' sake (Matthew 5:1, 3, 10)
3. sight (2 Corinthians 5:7 kjv)
4. on sand (Matthew 7:26)
5. b (Luke 19:11–26)

• • • • • • • • • • • •

1. True or False: Most of the Old Testament was originally written in the Hebrew language.

2. What special headwear will be the heavenly reward for faithful service on earth?

3. Connect the Thots:
   King David
   Moses
   Asaph

4. How old was Noah when God sent the flood to destroy the earth?

5. Match: Micah...
   a) son of Tekoa
   b) the shortest book of the minor prophets
   c) foretelling of a ruler to come from Bethlehem

Answers:

1. True
2. a crown (2 Timothy 4:8, James 1:12)
3. authors of Psalms (Psalm 3 niv; Psalm 90 niv; Psalm 73 niv)
4. six hundred (Genesis 7:11)
5. c (Micah 5:2)

1. In what kind of room did Jesus celebrate His last Passover with His disciples?

2. Connect the Thots:
   Wonderful
   Counsellor
   The Prince of Peace

3. Match: Jesus. . .
   a) promised rest for our souls.
   b) promised great material wealth to all believers.
   c) promised salvation based on good works alone.

4. What did Jesus say His love for Christians would be like?
   a) a man with his son
   b) a shepherd with his sheep
   c) a king with his queen
   d) a bear with her cub

5. What three-word title, later applied to Jesus Christ, did the voice of God use to address the prophet Ezekiel?

Quiz
78

1. What colorful garment did Joseph's father make for him?

2. Hannah named her son Samuel because
   a) she had promised the Lord she would.
   b) she had asked the Lord for him.
   c) she was told by God in a vision what to name him.
   d) Eli said that Samuel should be the boy's name.

3. What are the better-known names of Daniel's friends Hananiah, Mishael, and Azariah?

4. Samson's story can be found in
   a) The Acts of the Apostles.
   b) Judges.
   c) 2 Kings.
   d) 2 Chronicles.

5. Connect the Thots:
   Cyrus
   Darius
   Artaxerxes

Answers:

5. kings of Persia (Ezra 1:1; Ezra 4:5; Ezra 7:1)

4. b

3. Shadrach, Meshach, and Abednego (Daniel 1:7)

2. b (1 Samuel 1:20)

1. a coat of many colors (Genesis 37:3)

1. What did Jesus, in His first recorded miracle, change into wine?

2. Match: Creation...
   a) On the fourth day God filled the water with fish.
   b) On the third day God created sky as separate from water.
   c) On the third day God called the waters "seas."

3. True or False: Mary Magdalene was present at the crucifixion of Jesus Christ.

4. From what punishment did God save Daniel's three friends who refused to worship Nebuchadnezzar's statue?
   a) the lions' den
   b) forty lashes
   c) the fiery furnace
   d) drawing and quartering

5. Connect the Thots:
   water turned to blood
   dust turned to lice
   ashes turned to boils

Answers:

1. water (John 2:1–11)
2. c (Genesis 1:10, 13)
3. True (Matthew 27:50, 55–56)
4. c (Daniel 3:8–25)
5. plagues on Egypt (Exodus 7:14–19; Exodus 8:16–17; Exodus 9:8–12)

1. God corrects us because He
   a) will benefit.
   b) wants all Christians to be missionaries to the North Pole.
   c) wants us to learn how to be holy.
   d) thinks it is fun.

2. Fill in the blank:
   Jesus also calls the Counselor the Spirit of _____.

3. What did the Lord tell Samuel to do when Samuel saw David?

4. We can be separated from God's love by
   a) not going to church every Wednesday and Sunday.
   b) bad people.
   c) too much television.
   d) nothing.

5. What does the writer of Hebrews say we should continually offer to God?

Answers:

5. praise (Hebrews 13:15)
4. d (Romans 8:35–39)
3. The Lord told Samuel to anoint David king (1 Samuel 16:11–13).
2. truth (John 16:13)
1. c (Hebrews 12:10)

1. Who wrote the epistles to the Thessalonians?

2. What occupation did Joseph, Jesus' earthly father, practice?

3. Match: Demetrius...
   a) silversmith in Ephesus
   b) helper of Paul in Macedonia
   c) spokesman for Jews in Ephesus

4. What disciple was martyred by an angry, screaming crowd after a critical speech to the Sanhedrin?

5. Paul said he was Jewish so the Roman Christians would know that
   a) God has not forgotten His chosen people.
   b) Paul was better than the Roman Christians.
   c) Paul had paid handsomely to have a professional trace his family line.
   d) Paul was eligible to be a member of Boy Scouts.

Answers:

5. a (Romans 11:1–2)
4. Stephen (Acts 7:51–60)
3. a (Acts 19:24, 26)
2. carpentry (Matthew 13:53–55)
1. Paul the Apostle

1. What was the two-letter name of Job's homeland?

2. Connect the Thots:
   Fair Havens
   Syracuse
   Three Taverns

3. When Moses fled from Egypt, to what country did he go?

4. Match: Pool of Siloam. . .
   a) where Jesus sent a blind man
   b) where Jesus sent a demon-possessed man
   c) where Jesus sent a woman who was bleeding

5. What tribe of Israel, which could not occupy its allotted place in the Promised Land, took over somewhere else?

Answers:

1. Uz (Job 1:1)
2. stops on Paul's journey to Rome (Acts 27:1–8; Acts 28:12–14; Acts 28:14–15)
3. Midian (Exodus 2:15)
4. a (John 9:1–7)
5. Dan (Judges 18)

1. On the Sabbath, Jesus healed a man stricken with
   a) a withered hand.
   b) blindness.
   c) deafness.
   d) paralysis.

2. What three-word phrase did the resurrected Jesus repeat while reinstating Peter?

3. Match: Jesus. . .
   a) made no promises about the Holy Spirit.
   b) promised eternal life if we believe in Him.
   c) promised His coming would bring peace to families.

4. What great king of Israel did Jesus once quote from the book of Psalms?

5. Complete the scripture:
   Looking unto Jesus the _____ and finisher of our faith.

1. What weapon did David use to knock down the giant Goliath?
   a) a machine gun
   b) a bow and arrow
   c) a spear
   d) a sling

2. What moldable material, according to Jeremiah, represented Israel in the hands of God?

3. Isaiah prophesied of a time when the nations would beat their swords into what?
   a) plowshares
   b) anvils
   c) goblets
   d) the ground

4. What was the purpose for the three pairs of wings on the seraphim?

5. According to David, God's spiritual cleansing makes us whiter than what?
   a) dried bones
   b) snow
   c) clouds
   d) wool

Answers:

5. b (Psalm 51:7)
4. one set to cover their faces, one set to cover their feet, and one set to fly with (Isaiah 6:2)
3. a (Isaiah 2:4)
2. clay (Jeremiah 18:1–6)
1. d (1 Samuel 17:49–50)

1. What three words complete God's promise, "It is mine to avenge...," quoted by Paul in his letter to the Romans?

2. Connect the Thots:
   saying, "There is no God"
   despising a father's instruction
   trusting in one's self

3. True or False: Idolatry is the worship of false gods.

4. When Cain went out of the Lord's presence, he went to live in
   a) Mod.
   b) Nod.
   c) Sod.
   d) Cod.

5. What sin did the apostle Paul tell the Thessalonians is likely to occur at night?

Answers:

5. drunkenness (1 Thessalonians 5:7)

4. b (Genesis 4:16)

3. True

2. things relating to fools (Psalm 14:1; Proverbs 15:5; Proverbs 28:26)

1. I will repay (Romans 12:19 NIV).

Quiz
86

• • • • • • • • • • • •

1. What, according to Jesus, would set free the crowds who followed Him?

2. What does the apostle Paul, in the book of Romans, say Christians are *not* under, now that they are under grace?
   a) condemnation
   b) the flesh
   c) the law
   d) the curse

3. Complete this sentence:
   Jesus said that "with God all things are _____."

4. What *S* word, meaning "to yield," does James urge Christians to do to God?

5. Match: Parable of two men who prayed. . .
   a) The tax collector fasted once a week.
   b) The Pharisee fasted twice a week.
   c) The tax collector fasted twice a week.

Answers:

1. the truth (John 8:31–32)
2. c (Romans 6:14–15)
3. possible (Matthew 19:26)
4. submit (James 4:7)
5. b (Luke 18:9–13)

1. How many demons were cast out of Mary Magdalene?

2. Connect the Thots:
    shepherd
    green pastures
    a table "in the presence of mine enemies"

3. What five books of the Bible did Moses write?

4. Match: Malachi. . .
    a) After him, no prophet would speak
       God's voice for five hundred years.
    b) He wrote of the prophet Elijah's return.
    c) He wrote encouraging the rebuilding of the temple.

5. Why did Saul want to be soothed by music?

Answers:

1. seven (Luke 8:2)
2. Psalm 23 kjv
3. the Pentateuch—Genesis, Exodus, Leviticus, Numbers, Deuteronomy
4. b (Malachi 4:5)
5. because God had sent an evil spirit to bother rebellious Saul (1 Samuel 16:15–17)

1. Connect the Thots:
   the Jordan River
   "Thou art my beloved Son"
   John the Baptist

2. What four things did Jesus say "thou shalt love the Lord thy God with all thy"?

3. Complete the scripture:
   Who is he that overcometh the world, but he that believeth that Jesus is the _____ _____ _____?

4. How did Pilate's wife describe Jesus?

5. Match: Lamb of God...
   a) Jesus did not celebrate Passover the year He was crucified.
   b) Only Jesus as the Lamb was worthy to open the seven seals.
   c) Jesus was crucified by Himself.

Answers:

5. b (Revelation 5:5, 8)

4. a just or innocent man (Matthew 27:17–19)

3. Son of God (1 John 5:5 kjv)

2. heart, soul, mind, strength (Mark 12:30 kjv)

1. Jesus' baptism (Mark 1:4, 9–11 kjv)

1. What prophet went through an earthquake only to learn that God spoke in a gentle whisper?

2. When Satan placed boils on him, Job scratched them with
   a) broken pottery.
   b) his fingernails.
   c) the dull edge of a knife.
   d) the tip of a stick.

3. True or False: Rebekah gave Jacob the idea that he should deceive his father to steal Esau's blessing.

4. What wayward prophet actually complained that God is "a gracious God, and merciful, slow to anger, and of great kindness"?

5. Connect the Thots:
   son of Nun
   successor of Moses
   leader of Israel

Answers:

Quiz
90

• • • • • • • • • • • • •

1. What miraculous sign, interpreted by Daniel, foretold the doom of King Belshazzar?

2. Connect the Thots:
   Two witnesses are killed and resurrected in Jerusalem.
   Satan is bound for one thousand years.
   God wipes tears from believers' eyes.

3. Match: Crossing the Red Sea...
   a) God led the Hebrews through the wilderness to the Red Sea.
   b) Aaron carried the bones of Joseph across the Red Sea.
   c) Aaron stretched out his hand over the Red Sea.

4. True or False: The Feast of Trumpets took place to commemorate the seventh month.

5. What two people had time altered for them?

1. What was the first immediate effect on Jesus' disciples upon receiving the Holy Spirit?

2. No one will see God without
   a) a certificate of baptism.
   b) permission from St. Peter at the pearly gates.
   c) teaching Sunday School for twenty years.
   d) holiness.

3. Whom will you love if you also love God?

4. True or False: In Old Testament times, people never prayed directly to God.

5. Jesus says that God
   a) shows mercy only to those who love Him.
   b) remembers only those who thank Him for His goodness.
   c) is kind to everyone, including the evil and unthankful.
   d) will destroy our enemies if we ask Him.

Answers:

1. They began to speak in different languages (tongues) (Acts 1:13; 2:4).
2. d (Hebrews 12:14)
3. People who love God love their brother (1 John 4:21).
4. False (Genesis 24:12; 25:21; 1 Samuel 8:6; and many more!)
5. c (Luke 6:35)

Quiz
92

• • • • • • • • • • • •

1. Match: Paul, in Jerusalem...
   a) was transferred directly from there to Rome.
   b) was told by his nephew of a plot to kill him.
   c) preached at the site of an idol to an unknown god.

2. What missionary companion of Paul experienced an earthquake in a Philippian jail?

3. True or False: Because he was taken to Felix, Paul was rescued from certain death at the hands of more than forty Jews who opposed his teachings.

4. Whom did Paul say tried to keep him from making progress?

5. Gaius was
   a) a strong Christian who walked in the truth.
   b) a pagan John was trying to convert.
   c) one of the twelve disciples.
   d) a rich merchant who gave John millions of dollars to run his ministry.

1. Match: Valley of Elah. . .
   a) where Saul's army camped to meet Goliath
   b) where Solomon was made king
   c) where Satan tempted Jesus

2. What terrible locale, according to Jesus, is a place where "the fire is not quenched"?

3. Connect the Thots:
   Zin
   Paran
   Sinai

4. Where were the two disciples headed when Jesus walked with them after His resurrection?

5. What place did the Lord name that means "Is the Lord among us or not?"

1. Connect the Thots:
   the pure in heart
   the merciful
   they that mourn

2. How did Jesus describe the yoke He places on His followers?

3. Complete the scripture:
   As the Father hath loved me, so have I loved you: _____ ye in my love.

4. Who described Jesus as the "Lamb of God, who takes away the sin of the world"?

5. The adulteress's accusers interrupted Jesus as He was
   a) eating.
   b) praying.
   c) teaching.
   d) sleeping.

• • • • • • • • • • • •

1. What kind of animals rushed into a lake and drowned after receiving demons cast from humans?

2. Peter saw a vision that showed him it is permissible to
   a) eat food that had been sacrificed to idols.
   b) eat only animals considered clean under Jewish law.
   c) be a vegetarian.
   d) eat all kinds of animals.

3. What creatures did Jesus cite as having homes when "the Son of Man has no place to lay his head"?

4. Connect the Thots:
   the seven spirits of God before His throne
   "Thy word"
   five wise and five foolish virgins

5. What plague in Egypt came first, the frogs or the lice?

Answers:

1. pigs (Matthew 8:28–32)
2. d (Acts 10:9–18)
3. foxes and birds (Luke 9:58 NIV)
4. lamps (Revelation 4:5; Psalm 119:105 KJV; Matthew 25:1–13)
5. frogs (Exodus 8:5–17)

1. What extreme advice did Jesus have for a person whose "right hand offend thee"—indicating the seriousness of dealing with sin?

2. Jude was upset with ungodly men in the church because they
    a) did not give their full tithe.
    b) denied the Lord God and His Son Jesus Christ.
    c) sacrificed bulls instead of bullocks.
    d) spent all of the church's money on themselves.

3. What, according to James, is the source of every man's temptation?

4. Complete the scripture:
    And when the mourning was past, David sent and fetched her to his house, and she became his wife, and bare him a son. But the thing that David had done _____ the LORD.

5. Moneychangers were in the temple to
    a) provide correct change.
    b) exchange one form of money for another.
    c) drum up support.
    d) take bets on races in the Coliseum.

Answers:

5. b (John 2:13–16)
4. displeased (2 Samuel 11:27 kjv)
3. his own lust, or evil desire (James 1:14)
2. b (Jude 1:4)
1. cut it off (Matthew 5:30 kjv)

1. According to the Proverbs, a good wife wears
   a) plenty of red lipstick.
   b) the crown of life.
   c) joy unspeakable.
   d) strength and honor.

2. What type of person did Jesus use to contrast with the self-righteous Pharisees in a parable on humility?

3. Complete the scripture:
   For as the body without the spirit is _____, so faith without works is _____ also.

4. When someone wrongs you, what does Jesus say you should do first?

5. What was the apostle Peter's command regarding grace?
   a) remember
   b) share
   c) grow in
   d) pursue

1. Match: Amos. . .
    a) was shown a plumbline by God.
    b) was shown a bowl of spoiled fruit by God.
    c) was the son of a priest.

2. What did the apostle Paul say that long hair is to a woman?

3. Connect the Thots:
    bath
    cor
    homer

4. To what kind of weapon does the writer of Hebrews compare the Word of God?

5. The Law in the Pentateuch is often called the Mosaic Law because
    a) God gave the laws to Moses.
    b) all the laws are different, creating a "mosaic" of instructions.
    c) Moses broke the stone tablets and made up his own law.
    d) Moses was a police officer.

Answers:

5. a
4. double-edged sword (Hebrews 4:12 niv)
3. units of liquid measurement (Ezekiel 45:14)
2. glory (1 Corinthians 11:15)
1. a (Amos 7:8)

1. What is the Great Commission that Jesus gave His disciples before being taken up to heaven?

2. Jesus healed the Canaanite woman's daughter because
   a) her faith was great.
   b) He wanted to extend His ministry to the Gentiles.
   c) He wanted to show love for enemies.
   d) she washed His feet with perfume.

3. Connect the Thots:
   our Father
   our debts
   our daily bread

4. Jesus said, "Heaven and earth will pass away..." but what two-word answer would not?

5. A listing of Jesus' ancestors, or His lineage, is found
   a) in Matthew and Luke.
   b) in Mark and John.
   c) in Genesis and Revelation.
   d) in New York's Museum of Modern Art.

Answers:

5. a (Matthew 1:1–16; Luke 3:23–38)
4. My words (Matthew 24:35 NIV)
3. the Lord's Prayer (Matthew 6:9–13)
2. a (Matthew 15:21–28)
1. "Go into all the world and preach the good news to all creation" (Mark 16:15, 19 NIV)

• • • • • • • • • • • •

1. What woman lay at the feet of Boaz in a threshing floor—initiating a relationship that culminated in marriage?

2. True or False: Rachel, Leah, and their handmaids Zilpah and Bilhah were the mothers of the twelve tribes of Israel.

3. Connect the Thots:
   younger brother
   murder victim
   keeper of a flock

4. What Old Testament figure chose vegetables—or pulse—and water over his king's meat and wine?
   a) Moses
   b) Daniel
   c) David
   d) Jeremiah

5. Match: Hannah. . .
   a) Her husband, Elkanah, had no children.
   b) Eli the priest thought she was drunk.
   c) Eli's sons told her to leave the temple.

Answers:

5. b (1 Samuel 1:12–13)

4. b (Daniel 1:8–12)

3. Abel (Genesis 4:1–8)

2. True (Genesis 29:31–30:24; 35:16–18).

1. Ruth (Ruth 3:7–9; 4:13)

1. What transportation disaster befell the apostle Paul as he was traveling to Rome to stand trial before Caesar?

2. Match: Paul's shipwreck. . .
   a) occurred in the Mediterranean Sea.
   b) occurred in the Ionian Sea.
   c) occurred in the Adriatic Sea.

3. How many days did the Feast of Unleavened Bread last?

4. How did the Roman soldiers hasten the deaths of the robbers crucified with Jesus?
   a) by giving them poison
   b) by cutting off their heads
   c) by spearing them
   d) by breaking their legs

5. What bad man got his head nailed to the ground?

Answers:

1. shipwreck (Acts 27)
2. c (Acts 27:27, 41 NIV)
3. seven days (Exodus 12:18–19)
4. d (John 19:32)
5. Sisera (Judges 4:2–3, 17, 21)

1. How did God show His presence at the dedication of Solomon's temple?

2. Fill in the blank:
   Paul writes in 2 Corinthians that we praise a "Father of compassion and the God of all _____."

3. According to the Proverbs, a gentle answer turns away what?
   a) wrath
   b) enemies
   c) arguments
   d) lawsuits

4. True or False: God did not have any special consideration for the poor until Jesus spoke about them in the New Testament.

5. What is the first of God's Ten Commandments?

Answers:

5. "Thou shalt have no other gods before me" (Exodus 20:3 kjv).

4. False. Many of God's Old Testament laws contained provisions for the poor.

3. a (Proverbs 15:1 niv)

2. comfort (2 Corinthians 1:3 niv)

1. Fire came down from heaven and consumed the sacrifices; God's glory filled the place (2 Chronicles 6:10, 12; 7:1).

1. According to Jesus, who will inherit the earth?
    a) the environmentalists
    b) the merciful
    c) the peacemakers
    d) the meek

2. What notorious prisoner gained his freedom from Pontius Pilate as Jesus was sentenced to crucifixion?

3. Connect the Thots:
    Amplias
    Nymphas
    Andronicus

4. What nationality, hated by the Jews, provided the "good guy" character in Jesus' parable of a man beaten by robbers?

5. Match: Zechariah. . .
    a) was told by the angel to name his son John.
    b) received the message from the angel Michael.
    c) was visited by the angel at his home in Jerusalem.

1. What mountain was the setting for Moses's encounter with God in a burning bush?

2. Connect the Thots:
   Jabbok
   Ulai
   Kishon

3. Toward the end of his life, Jeremiah was taken captive to what country?

4. Match: The new Jerusalem. . .
   a) has no temple.
   b) has a sun and moon.
   c) has gates that close at night.

5. From what location did Moses send the twelve spies into the Promised Land?

Answers:

1. Horeb (Exodus 3:1–6)
2. rivers (Deuteronomy 3:16; Daniel 8:2 kjv; Judges 5:21)
3. Egypt (Jeremiah 43:1–7)
4. a (Revelation 21)
5. wilderness of Paran (Numbers 13:1–17)

Quiz
105

1. To whom did Jesus first appear following His resurrection?

2. The two sources that trace Jesus' lineage differ from David to Jesus. This is because
   a) neither one is accurate.
   b) the records in Bethlehem burned.
   c) one source had to guess at names after a computer crash.
   d) one traces Joseph's line from David, while the other traces Mary's ancestors.

3. Seated on the throne in the book of Revelation, Jesus tells the disciple John, "I am making everything _____!"

4. Connect the Thots:
   the meek
   the poor in spirit
   the peacemakers

5. According to Paul, how was Jesus in the wilderness with Moses and the children of Israel?

Answers:

5. as the spiritual Rock that followed them (1 Corinthians 10:1–4)

4. people Jesus blessed in His Beatitudes (Matthew 5:1–10)

3. new (Revelation 21:2–5 NIV)

2. d

1. Mary Magdalene and another Mary (Matthew 28)

1. What swarming insects stripped Egypt of every green plant in the eighth plague called down by Moses?

2. Who is known as the "father of all who play the harp"?
   a) David
   b) Jubal
   c) Seth
   d) Asaph

3. To what animals did Jesus liken His disciples and the unbelievers to whom they would be sent?

4. What kind of branches did people spread before Jesus during His "triumphal entry" into Jerusalem?
   a) olive
   b) oak
   c) palm
   d) sycamore

5. To what creature did God say, "I will put enmity between thee and the woman"?

Answers:

5. the serpent (Genesis 3:14–15 kjv)
4. c (John 12:12–13)
3. sheep among wolves (Matthew 10:16)
2. b (Genesis 4:21 niv)
1. locusts (Exodus 10:13–15)

1. What two disciples let their anger get the best of them by suggesting that a Samaritan village that had snubbed Jesus be destroyed by fire from heaven?

2. How did Jesus respond to His disciples' comment above?
   a) He wept.
   b) He rebuked them.
   c) He prayed.
   d) He ignored them.

3. What false goddess, called by some "the queen of heaven," was pursued by Solomon?

4. Complete the scripture:
   Your iniquities have separated between you and your God, and your sins have hid his face from you, that he will not _____.

5. Why were the children of Israel condemned to wander in the wilderness for forty years?

Answers:

1. James and John (Luke 9:50–54)
2. b (Luke 9:55–56)
3. Ashtoreth (1 Kings 11:5)
4. hear (Isaiah 59:2 kjv)
5. because they refused to conquer the Promised Land when God told them (Numbers 14)

Quiz
108

• • • • • • • • • • • • •

1. What attitude of giving, according to the apostle Paul, does God love?

2. Complete the scripture:
   Grow in grace, and in the _____ of our Lord and Saviour Jesus Christ.

3. Which of Paul's letters includes the famous charge, "Study to shew thyself approved unto God"?

4. Another name for Jesus' Sermon on the Mount is
   a) Beatitudes.
   b) Attitude Adjustments.
   c) Beatniks.
   d) Assertiveness Training.

5. When a good woman speaks, what do her words have?

Answers:

1. cheerful (2 Corinthians 9:7)
2. knowledge (2 Peter 3:18 kjv)
3. 2 Timothy (2:15 kjv)
4. a
5. wisdom (Proverbs 31:10, 26)

1. A psalter
   a) sprinkles salt.
   b) fights wild animals.
   c) copies manuscripts.
   d) sings praises to God.

2. What son of David cut his long hair whenever it became too heavy for him?

3. Connect the Thots:
   the rainfall of Noah's flood
   Jesus' fast in the wilderness
   Jesus' post-resurrection appearances

4. Match: Nahum. . .
   a) predicted Babylon's doom.
   b) predicted Nineveh's destruction.
   c) predicted fifty more prosperous years for Nineveh.

5. What is the last book of the New Testament?

1. Complete the scripture:
Then said Jesus, Father, _____ them; for they know not what they do.

2. On two occasions, Jesus is recorded as feeding crowds numbering in the thousands. How many were in each crowd?

3. What did Jesus say would not prevail against His church?
    a) the sins of mankind
    b) the armies of Satan
    c) the gates of Hades
    d) the forces of evil

4. What *S* word completes Jesus' sentence: "I desire mercy, not _____."

5. True or False: Jesus doubted the sincerity of Zacchaeus's repentance.

Answers:

1. forgive (Luke 23:34 kjv)
2. Five thousand men, plus women and children; and four thousand men, plus women and children (Matthew 14:13–21; 15:32–38)
3. c (Matthew 16:17–18)
4. sacrifice (Matthew 12:7 niv)
5. False (Luke 19:8–9)

1. What woman was Jacob tricked into marrying by his devious uncle Laban?

2. Connect the Thots:
   King Eglon of Moab
   King Joash of Judah
   King Sennacherib of Assyria

3. Who were Miriam's brothers?

4. Complete the scripture:
   "_____ came I out of my mother's womb, and _____ shall I return thither: the LORD gave, and the LORD hath taken away; blessed be the name of the LORD."

5. Hagar was
   a) a handmaid.
   b) an Egyptian.
   c) the mother of Ishmael as a result of Sarah's decision.
   d) all of the above.

Answers:

1. Leah (Genesis 29:13, 21–25)
2. victims of assassination (Judges 3:12–25; 2 Kings 12:19–20; 2 Kings 19:36–37)
3. Aaron and Moses (1 Chronicles 6:3)
4. naked, naked (Job 1:21 kjv)
5. d (Genesis 16:1, 3–11)

Quiz
112

• • • • • • • • • •

1. The Feast of Unleavened Bread began
   a) the day after Passover.
   b) the day before Passover.
   c) on Moses's birthday.
   d) when everyone ran out of yeast.

2. Which day of creation included God making night?

3. Connect the Thots:
   the feeding of five thousand
   the healing of Jairus's daughter
   an unexpected catch of fish

4. What did Heber's wife, Jael, do that made her famous?

5. Match: The flood. . .
   a) Noah was five hundred years old when the flood came.
   b) Noah took seven pairs of every clean animal onto the ark.
   c) The waters flooded the earth for fifty days.

Answers:

5. b (Genesis 7:1–2, 5)
4. She nailed a man's head to the ground (Judges 4:21).
3. miracles of Jesus (Matthew 14:13–21; Mark 5:22–42; Luke 5:1–6)
2. the first (Genesis 1:5)
1. a (Numbers 28:16–17)

1. What is the Aramaic word for "father" or "daddy"?

2. To show us His love, God
   a) sent his only begotten Son into the world, that we might live through Him.
   b) sent manna to all Christians.
   c) promised vast wealth to all Christians.
   d) promised that one day we would have pictures of Mars.

3. Who has not seen God?

4. True or False: The "Father's house" is another way of saying heaven.

5. What name for Himself does God say He used when appearing to Abraham, Isaac, and Jacob?

Answers:

1. Abba (Romans 8:15)
2. a (1 John 4:9)
3. people who do evil (3 John 11)
4. True (John 14:2)
5. God Almighty (Exodus 6:3)

1. What synagogue official saw his twelve-year-old daughter raised to life by Jesus?

2. True or False: Felix was married to a Jewess named Drusilla.

3. Who asked Jesus to let the sons of Zebedee sit at each side of Jesus in His kingdom?

4. Connect the Thots:
   Jesus in Samaria
   a request for a drink
   five husbands

5. Match: Joseph, husband of Mary. . .
   a) He was not a direct descendant of David.
   b) The seer Simeon told him to flee to Egypt with Jesus.
   c) He wanted to obtain a divorce from Mary.

1. Of the four rivers that were said to flow from the Garden of Eden, what two share names with important rivers of the modern Middle East?

2. Connect the Thots:
   Ephesus
   Smyrna
   Thyatira

3. What town was home to Zacchaeus?

4. Match: Gaza...
   a) where Samson asked to die with the Philistines
   b) where Samson met his wife
   c) a city of Benjamin

5. Where was Eve in the Garden of Eden when the serpent spoke to her?

Answers:

1. Tigris and Euphrates (Genesis 2:10–14)
2. churches of Revelation (Revelation 2:1; Revelation 2:8; Revelation 2:18)
3. Jericho (Luke 19:1–6)
4. a (Judges 16:20–30)
5. in the center (Genesis 2:9; 3:6)

1. Daniel refers to Jesus as the "Ancient of _____"?

2. What did certain Jews call Jesus after He proclaimed, "If anyone keeps my word, he will never see death"?

3. True or False: John wrote down everything that Jesus did.

4. What Roman official asked Jesus to heal his servant?
    a) a centurion
    b) a general
    c) a proconsul
    d) a governor

5. Connect the Thots:
    James the son of Alphaeus
    Simon the Canaanite
    Thomas

1. What musical instrument did Miriam, Aaron's sister, play?
   a) horn
   b) harp
   c) flute
   d) tambourine

2. What substance did God use to form the first man?

3. Connect the Thots:
   Jonah's plant
   Herod's death
   hell's immortal creatures

4. What ravenous animal would feed peacefully with the lamb in the new earth prophesied by Isaiah?

5. What did Paul suggest Timothy should take for his frequent illnesses?
   a) wine
   b) cheese
   c) honey
   d) herbs

Answers:

5. a (1 Timothy 5:23)
4. wolf (Isaiah 65:18, 25)
3. worms (Jonah 4:6–8; Acts 12:21–23; Mark 9:44–46)
2. dust (Genesis 2:7 NIV)
1. d (Exodus 15:20)

1. What king of Assyria insulted God to King Hezekiah of Judah—and paid for it with his life?

2. What did a seraph touch to Isaiah's lips to take away his guilt and sin?
   a) a golden bowl
   b) a budding pole
   c) a live coal
   d) a sealed scroll

3. What false prophet prophesied against Jeremiah and died?

4. When Jonah tried to escape God's will, he
   a) was swallowed by a big fish.
   b) proved successful in his attempt to escape.
   c) told God he would go to Nineveh if He would name a Bible book after him.
   d) wrote a book called *Jonah's Travels.*

5. Complete the scripture:
   If we claim to be without sin, we _____ ourselves and the truth is not in us.

Answers:

5. deceive (1 John 1:8 NIV)
4. a (Jonah 1)
3. Hananiah (Jeremiah 28)
2. c (Isaiah 6:6–7)
1. Sennacherib (2 Kings 19:5–13, 35–37)

1. What is more important than beauty in a good woman?

2. Jesus said to store your treasures in
   a) the stock market.
   b) other people.
   c) real estate.
   d) heaven.

3. What did the apostle Paul say is profitable, or useful, for teaching, rebuking, correcting, and training in righteousness?

4. Complete the scripture:
   Bear ye one another's burdens, and so _____ the law of Christ.

5. In a parable describing the kingdom of heaven, where did Jesus say a man found a hidden treasure?

Answers:

5. in a field (Matthew 13:44)
4. fulfil (Galatians 6:2 kjv)
3. scripture (2 Timothy 3:16)
2. d (Matthew 6:20)
1. fear of the Lord (Proverbs 31:30)

1. Match: Zephaniah...
   a) wrote during the reign of King Josiah.
   b) was the son of Pethuel.
   c) wrote during the reign of King Uzziah.

2. What Philistine idol fell over and broke in pieces when the ark of the covenant was placed nearby?

3. Connect the Thots:
   Naaman at the Jordan River
   Pontius Pilate's hands
   Jesus and the disciples' feet

4. A prophet is
   a) an astronomer.
   b) a psychic.
   c) one who interprets dreams.
   d) one sent by God to tell His plans for the future.

5. How many of Peter's letters are included in the Bible?

1. Who did Jesus tell an expert in the Law he should love as himself?

2. Complete this scripture from Matthew describing Jesus: I will open my mouth in parables, I will utter things hidden since _____ _____ _____ _____ _____.

3. Like Daniel, in the book of Revelation, John describes Jesus as having hair of what color?

4. Connect the Thots:
   a withered hand made well
   a fig tree cursed
   a coin found in a fish's mouth

5. What were Jesus' last words on the cross?

Quiz
122

1. What nationality of woman did Samson, to his parents' disgust, seek out for a wife?

2. Mephiboseth was
    a) blind.
    b) lame in both feet.
    c) a leper.
    d) deaf.

3. Connect the Thots:
    Ahinoam
    Abigail
    Michal

4. Match: Elizabeth...
    a) Mary stayed with her for six months.
    b) Her husband regained his sight at their son's birth.
    c) Her husband said their son would be a prophet.

5. Who was Cain and Abel's brother?

Answers:

5. Seth (Genesis 4:25)
4. c (Luke 1:63, 67, 76)
3. wives of King David (1 Samuel 30:5; 1 Samuel 19:11)
2. b (2 Samuel 9:13)
1. Philistine (Judges 14:1–3)

1. What did scoffers accuse the disciples of when they spoke in tongues at Pentecost?

2. Connect the Thots:
   Jesus' ascension into heaven
   the Holy Spirit's arrival at Pentecost
   the deaths of Ananias and Sapphira

3. Match: Siege of Jerusalem...
   a) described by Ezekiel in words God gave him
   b) ended by Ezekiel putting on ashes and sackcloth
   c) depicted by model Ezekiel built

4. How many days did the people celebrate following the completion of Solomon's temple?

5. What annual occasion witnessed the priest using the scapegoat?

1. What name did Jesus use for the Holy Spirit?

2. Fill in the blank:
   Jesus tells us that in His Father's house are many _____.

3. When we go to God in prayer, we should
      a) be humble.
      b) convince Him how great we are.
      c) give Him a list of our accomplishments in church.
      d) tell Him all about the latest Star Wars movie.

4. What name of God, which is *El-Elyon* in Hebrew,
   was used to describe the God whom the high priest
   Melchizedek served?

5. Who tried to buy the gifts of the Holy Spirit?

Answers:

1. Comforter (kjv), Counselor (niv) (John 15:26)
2. rooms (niv) or mansions (kjv) (John 14:2)
3. a (2 Chronicles 7:14)
4. most high God (Genesis 14:18 kjv)
5. Simon the sorcerer (Acts 8:9, 18–19)

1. What devout man held the baby Jesus when Mary and Joseph presented Him at the temple?

2. Connect the Thots:
   James the son of Zebedee
   Thaddaeus
   Bartholomew

3. The repentant criminal who was crucified with Jesus asked Him to
   a) remember him.
   b) reward him for defending Him against the other criminal.
   c) save him.
   d) be buried with him.

4. Match: Mary, earthly mother of Jesus...
   a) She and Joseph offered a pair of goats when they presented Jesus at the temple courts.
   b) She received a blessing from Simeon.
   c) She received a blessing from the prophetess Anna.

5. Who was the first person killed because he believed in Christ?

Answers:

5. Stephen (Acts 7:56–60)

4. b (Luke 2:34)

3. a (Luke 23:39–42)

2. disciples of Jesus (Matthew 10:2–4)

1. Simeon (Luke 2:25–32)

Quiz
126

• • • • • • • • • • • •

1. What lodging place in Bethlehem turned away Joseph and his very expectant wife, Mary?

2. Peter wrote his first letter to the elect in
   a) Pontus and Galatia.
   b) Asia.
   c) Cappadocia and Bithynia.
   d) all of the above.

3. Match: Hebron. . .
   a) where Lot chose to live
   b) where Abimelech and Abraham swore an oath
   c) near the Cave of Machpelah

4. What was the "great city," or capital, of Assyria?

5. What did Jonah do inside the giant fish?
   a) practice karate
   b) pray
   c) cry
   d) build a fire

Answers:

5. b (Jonah 2:1)
4. Nineveh (Genesis 10:11–12 NIV; Jonah 3:3)
3. c (Genesis 23:1–2, 19)
2. d (1 Peter 1:1–2)
1. inn (Luke 2:4–7)

Quiz
127

1. What two *W* words did Jesus' disciples utter when they said, "Who is this? Even the _____ and the _____ obey him"?

2. True or False: The Bible tells us Jesus had an active prayer life.

3. Jesus often prayed
   a) loudly, so all would hear.
   b) alone.
   c) only with His disciples, or else others would learn how to pray
   d) only in church.

4. Complete the scripture:
   "Abba, _____ ," he said, "everything is _____ for you. Take this cup from me. Yet not what I _____, but what you _____ ."

5. What troublemaking religious leaders—accusing Jesus of casting out demons by the prince of demons—had their thoughts read by Jesus?

Answers:

1. wind, waves (Mark 4:40–41 NIV)
2. True (see Mark 1:35 as one example)
3. b (Luke 5:16)
4. Father, possible, will, will (Mark 14:6 NIV)
5. Pharisees (Matthew 12:22–28)

Quiz
128

1. What kind of animals helped Samson burn the grain fields of his enemies?
   a) lightning bugs
   b) lions
   c) donkeys
   d) foxes

2. What kind of bird, released from the ark, brought an olive leaf back to Noah?

3. Connect the Thots:
   Arcturus (the Bear)
   Orion
   Pleiades

4. What animal were the Israelites not to muzzle as it was treading grain (NIV), or corn (KJV)?

5. What did Peter see inside a sheet, coming down from heaven by its four corners?
   a) animals, reptiles, and birds
   b) gold and silver
   c) people of many countries
   d) Christmas presents

Answers:

5. a (Acts 10:9–12)
4. ox (Deuteronomy 25:4)
3. constellations (Job 9:9)
2. dove (Genesis 8:11)
1. d (Judges 15:3–5)

1. The Lord told Job's visitors that He was
   a) pleased with them.
   b) willing to prosper them.
   c) angry that they were unsuccessful at teaching Job
      new skills.
   d) angry about their unfaithfulness to Him.

2. What excuse did Adam give for hiding when he heard
   God's voice?

3. A true prophet
   a) always has good news.
   b) is not always sent from God.
   c) works for profit.
   d) often is sent to warn God's people to repent of sin.

4. What horrible thing did Athaliah do?

5. Connect the Thots:
   scribes and Pharisees
   blind guides
   Chorazin and Bethsaida

Answers:

1. d (Job 42:7)
2. afraid, naked (either answer acceptable) (Genesis 3:9–10)
3. d
4. killed her grandchildren so she could be queen (2 Kings 11:1–3 kjv)
5. "woe" pronounced by Jesus (Luke 11:44; Matthew 23:16; Luke 10:13 kjv)

1. What will happen to the woman who fears the Lord?

2. What did Jesus say He came to call sinners to?

3. Complete the scripture:
   Trust in the LORD with all thine heart; and _____ not unto thine own understanding.

4. James writes that anyone who listens to the Word and does not do what it says is like a man who does what?

5. Connect the Thots:
   the Pharisee and the publican, or tax collector
   the rich man and Lazarus
   the lost sheep

1. True or False: Women judges were common in the Old Testament.

2. What four-word phrase is used often in the book of Isaiah to describe the Lord?

3. Connect the Thots:
   a parabolic Pharisee, twice a week
   Queen Esther's Jews, for three days
   Jesus, for forty days

4. What part of the body, according to James, "can no man tame"?

5. Match: Joel. . .
   a) son of Pethuel
   b) son of Tekoa
   c) son of Obadiah

1. What did the terrified disciples think they were seeing when Jesus walked across the water to their boat?

2. True or False: Every spirit that does not acknowledge Jesus is not from God.

3. When Jesus sent forth His twelve disciples the first time, what did He give them the power and authority to do?

4. Complete the scripture:
   "Whoever welcomes this little child in my name welcomes ___."

5. Only Matthew records Jesus' encounter with two blind men. What do they call Jesus?

Answers:

5. Son of David (Matthew 9:27)
4. me (Luke 9:48 NIV)
3. power and authority over all demons and to cure diseases (Luke 9:1)
2. True (1 John 4:3 NIV)
1. a ghost, or spirit (Matthew 14:22-27)

1. What daughter did Reuel, a priest of Midian, give to Moses as his wife?

2. What otherwise faithful man once had an embarrassing episode of drunkenness in his tent?
   a) Moses
   b) Joshua
   c) Joseph
   d) Noah

3. Connect the Thots:
   the sons—or descendants—of Anak
   Ishbibenob
   Goliath

4. Match: Hagar. . .
   a) She was Abram's first wife.
   b) She and Sarai were half sisters.
   c) She ran away from Sarai.

5. Abraham and Sarah didn't want their son Isaac to marry any of the local women because they were
   a) Canaanites.
   b) Israelites.
   c) members of the Electric Light Orchestra.
   d) ugly.

Answers:

5. a (Genesis 24:1–3)
4. c (Genesis 16:8)
3. giants (Numbers 13:33; 2 Samuel 21:16 kjv; 1 Samuel 17:4)
2. d (Genesis 9:20–21)
1. Zipporah (Exodus 2:16–21)

1. How many leprous men came to Jesus requesting a mass healing—for which only one returned to praise God?

2. Connect the Thots:
   light
   heaven
   earth

3. What Old Testament feast was celebrated every month?

4. Match: The Lord's Supper. . .
   a) Bread represented manna in the wilderness.
   b) Bread represented Jesus' body.
   c) Bread represented the bread of the Presence in the tabernacle.

5. How often did the year of Jubilee occur?

Answers:

5. every fifty years (Leviticus 25:10)
4. b (Mark 14:22)
3. Feast of the New Moon (1 Samuel 20:5)
2. the first three days of Creation (Genesis 1:1–13)
1. ten (Luke 17:11–19)

1. What did Jesus tell the disciples that the Holy Spirit would specifically do?

2. Fill in the blank:
Only Jesus has seen the _____, since He is from God.

3. The Lord spoke to Zechariah through
    a) visions.
    b) a book.
    c) the Lord's web page.
    d) dreams.

4. After Pentecost, how did the apostles impart the Holy Spirit?

5. According to John, what does the Holy Spirit help us do?

Answers:

1. abide with them forever (John 14:15–17)
2. Father (John 6:46)
3. a
4. by the laying on of hands (Acts 8:14–17)
5. test the spirits (1 John 4:1–3)

Quiz
136

1. John said Demetrius was godly because he
   a) did not like Diotrephes.
   b) praised all of John's epistles.
   c) was a true Christian witness.
   d) gave John fine food and lodging.

2. What forbidden art did a Simon from Samaria practice before he accepted Christ?

3. Connect the Thots:
   Didymus
   doubting the Resurrection
   "My Lord and my God"

4. Match: Mary and Martha. . .
   a) Martha met Jesus when he arrived after Lazarus's death.
   b) Mary was known to busy herself with household chores.
   c) Mary preferred to sit with Jesus rather than to help Martha.

5. True or False: Another name for Jesus' mother is Mary Magdalene.

Answers:

1. c (3 John 12)
2. sorcery (Acts 8:9–24)
3. the apostle Thomas (John 20:24–28)
4. c (Luke 10:38–40; John 11:1–44)
5. False. Mary Magdalene was one of Jesus' followers (Luke 8:1–2).

1. In what town did Elijah bring a widow's son back to life?

2. Connect the Thots:
   a post-flood migration
   a confusion of languages
   a tower to heaven

3. From what mountain was Moses given a look into the Promised Land?

4. Match: Valley of Jezreel...
   a) where David was anointed by Samuel
   b) where Hannah dedicated Samuel to the Lord
   c) where opposing armies were camped to meet Gideon

5. Where did the valiant men bury Saul's bones?

Answers:

1. Zarephath (1 Kings 17:8–22)
2. Babel (Genesis 10:32–11:9)
3. Mount Nebo (Deuteronomy 32:48–49)
4. c (Judges 6:33–35)
5. under a tree at Jabesh (1 Samuel 31:12–13)

1. When Jesus cried on the cross, "My God, my God, why have you forsaken me?" He was repeating a line from what Old Testament book?

2. Connect the Thots:
   Son of Man
   Son of David
   Son of God

3. What famous half brother could a certain Simon, with his full brothers James, Joseph, and Judas, claim?

4. Complete this scripture spoken by Jesus of the Samaritan who was a good neighbor:
   "Go and do _____."

5. How did Jesus at age twelve refer to the temple in Jerusalem?

1. What judge of Israel had thirty sons who rode thirty donkeys?
   a) Tola
   b) Jair
   c) Jephthah
   d) Eli

2. What color-changing lizard was not permitted on Israelite menus?

3. Connect the Thots:
   a cloke (cloak)
   books
   parchments

4. What noisemakers hung off the hem of the priest's garment?

5. Match: Ravens...
   a) fed Elisha by the Jordan River.
   b) fed Noah on Mount Ararat.
   c) fed Elijah by the Kerith Ravine.

1. An angry man
    a) is a victim of his surroundings.
    b) should be put on the welfare rolls.
    c) stirs up even more anger.
    d) should be allowed to get away with anything he
       wants.

2. What forbidden tree in the Garden of Eden did the
   serpent convince Eve to eat from?

3. What disguise does Satan use to try to fool
   Christians?
    a) a passionate preacher
    b) a wounded traveler
    c) an angel of light
    d) an innocent child

4. Who was cursed with pain in childbirth?

5. A person who will not listen to wise advice will find
    a) poverty and shame.
    b) health and wealth.
    c) his own wisdom.
    d) a new job.

Answers:

5. a (Proverbs 13:18)
4. Eve (Genesis 3:16–20)
3. c (2 Corinthians 11:14)
2. the tree of the knowledge of good and evil (Genesis 2:15–17; 3:1–6)
1. c (Proverbs 29:22)

1. Which day of the week did the apostle Paul tell believers to put aside money for their offerings?

2. Connect the Thots:
   your parents
   better than sacrifice
   God rather than men

3. In Jesus' illustration, what does the man do who loses one sheep out of one hundred?

4. As to our gifts from God, Paul said
   a) all Christians have equal gifts.
   b) we should go to classes to develop our gifts.
   c) that for a small fee, he would help the Romans find their gifts.
   d) we should use whatever gifts God gave us.

5. What is the popular name for Jesus' command to do unto others as you would have them to unto you?

Answers:

5. the Golden Rule (see Matthew 7:12)

4. d (Romans 12:3–8)

3. leaves the ninety-nine other sheep and goes to look for that one (Matthew 18:1, 12)

2. obey (Ephesians 6:1; 1 Samuel 15:22; Acts 5:29)

1. the first day (1 Corinthians 16:1–2)

1. True or False: In Deborah's time, Israel was a free nation.

2. What body fluid was part of the curse that came by Adam and Eve's sin?

3. Connect the Thots:
   Paul
   Achan
   Stephen

4. What kind of lion does the apostle Peter compare the devil to?

5. Match: Fourteen...
   a) years Samson was judge of Israel
   b) number of original children of Job
   c) generations from Abraham to David

Answers:

5. c (Matthew 1:17)
4. roaring (1 Peter 5:8)
3. people who were stoned (Acts 14:19; Joshua 7:24–26; Acts 7:59)
2. sweat (Genesis 3:19)
1. False (Judges 4:1–4)

Quiz
143

1. What civic duty did the chief priests and scribes hope to use to get Jesus in trouble with Caesar?

2. Connect the Thots:
   "Hosanna"
   "Hail, King of the Jews!"
   "Crucify him"

3. To whom did Jesus say, "I tell you the truth, today you will be with me in paradise"?

4. What event did Jesus use as an example to emphasize the need for repentance?
   a) an earthquake in Jerusalem
   b) a tower collapse that killed eighteen people
   c) an outbreak of the plague
   d) the drowning of seven people in a boat accident

5. What name for Jesus, meaning "Anointed One," did the angel of the Lord use when speaking to the shepherds?

Answers:

5. Christ (Luke 2:8–11)
4. b (Luke 13:2–5)
3. one of the criminals crucified with Him (Luke 23:39–43 NIV)
Luke 23:21)
2. things people shouted at Jesus (John 12:12–13; Matthew 27:27–29;
1. paying taxes (Luke 20:19-26)

1. What intelligent and beautiful woman, the wife of the surly Nabal, married King David after Nabal died?

2. What did David take from an unsuspecting King Saul, rather than killing him as David's men urged?
   a) a lock of his hair
   b) a corner of his robe
   c) an arrow from his quiver
   d) a strap from his sandal

3. What term describes Samson, who was never to cut his hair?

4. Connect the Thots:
   a drinking party
   handwriting on a wall
   knocking knees

5. Match: Joseph. . .
   a) He dreamed of a vine with three branches that budded.
   b) He wore his coat of many colors in Pharaoh's palace.
   c) He dreamed his brothers bowed down to him.

Answers:

5. c (Genesis 37:5, 9–10)
4. King Belshazzar (Daniel 5:1–6)
3. Nazirite (Judges 13)
2. b (1 Samuel 24:1–11)
1. Abigail (1 Samuel 25:3, 39–42)

1. How quickly will the glorification of the saints, announced by "the last trumpet," take place?
    a) in the twinkling of an eye
    b) as a horse gallops
    c) in a heartbeat
    d) as the eagle swoops

2. Connect the Thots:
    using spit to heal a blind man
    raising Lazarus to life
    walking on water

3. What was the name of the angel who told Mary she would give birth to Jesus?
    a) Michael
    b) Zadok
    c) Gabriel
    d) Hananiah

4. Match: First Passover. . .
    a) raisin cakes
    b) barley bread
    c) bread without yeast

5. Which one of Joseph's brothers kept his other brothers from killing Joseph?
    a) Judah
    b) Benjamin
    c) Dan
    d) Reuben

Answers:

5. d (Genesis 37:17–21)
4. c (Exodus 12:8, 11)
3. c (Luke 1:26–31)
2. miracles of Jesus (Mark 8:22–25; John 11:38–44, Mark 6:45–50)
1. a (1 Corinthians 15:51–52 NIV)

1. Around whom does the angel of the Lord encamp?

2. Complete this scripture from the book of Hebrews:
   For every house is built by someone, but God is the
   builder of _____.

3. How did the Holy Spirit empower Moses's seventy
   elders?

4. According to James, what should a tempted person never
   say?
   a) "The devil made me do it."
   b) "My own strength shall save me."
   c) "It is of little account."
   d) "God is tempting me."

5. According to Zephaniah 3:17, how does God feel about
   His people?

1. The Bible tells of a Pharisee who prayed
   a) loudly, boasting about his goodness.
   b) silently.
   c) in French, a language unheard of at that time.
   d) for God to have mercy upon him.

2. Which apostle defended himself before a king named Agrippa—and tried to convert him in the process?

3. True or False: The crowds were pleased by the prospect of Jesus dining with Zacchaeus.

4. Match: Paul. . .
   a) An angel told him he would not stand trial in Rome.
   b) An angel told him only two lives would be lost in a shipwreck.
   c) An angel told him all on board ship would be saved.

5. What religious and political entity, whose name means "sitting together," tried to find false evidence against Jesus?

Answers:

1. a (Luke 18:11)
2. Paul (Acts 25:13–26:28)
3. False (Luke 19:5–7)
4. c (Acts 27:23–24)
5. Sanhedrin (Matthew 26:59 NIV)

1. When Moses died, in what land did God bury him?

2. What river divided when the prophet Elisha struck it with Elijah's cloak?

3. Connect the Thots:
   Tarshish
   Joppa
   Nineveh

4. In what town did Jesus encounter a widow who had lost her only son?

5. What was the potter's field also known as?

1. Which of the following sounds will not accompany Jesus' Second Coming?
   a) the trumpet of God
   b) mighty hoof beats
   c) the voice of the archangel
   d) a loud command

2. The shortest verse in the Bible, "Jesus wept," occurs during the telling of what story?

3. Complete the scripture:
   For the Son of man is come to seek and to save that which was _____.

4. Did Jesus know He was to be crucified?

5. Complete Jesus' statement about human souls:
   "The harvest is plentiful. . .
   a) and the time is short.
   b) but the workers are few.
   c) for the Lord has blessed.
   d) with the choicest of fruit.

Answers:

5. b (Matthew 9:37 niv)
4. yes (Matthew 20:17–19)
3. lost (Luke 19:10 kjv)
2. the raising of Lazarus from the dead (John 11:35 niv)
1. b (1 Thessalonians 4:16 niv)

Quiz
150

1. What soaring bird, mentioned in Isaiah 40, led Moses's list of flying creatures that could not be eaten?

2. Connect the Thots:
   cucumbers
   melons
   leeks

3. How many swords did the disciples take with them when they followed Jesus to the Garden of Gethsemane?

4. Match: Manna. . .
   a) stopped the day after the Israelites ate the bread of Canaan.
   b) tasted like quail.
   c) continued until the Israelites conquered Jericho.

5. Who will judge the angels?

Quiz
151

1. What sin of David led to a plague that killed seventy thousand Israelites?
   a) his adultery with Bathsheba
   b) the murder of Uriah
   c) counting the Israelites
   d) polygamy

2. What *W* word does Paul use in Romans 7 to describe himself when torn between doing good and evil?

3. Connect the Thots:
   You'll be proven a liar.
   You'll receive plagues.
   You'll lose your part in the book of life.

4. What two descriptions of Satan appear in Revelation 12:9?

5. How did Samuel know that Saul had disobeyed God by failing to completely annihilate the Amalekites?
   a) Saul's shifty eyes
   b) the sound of livestock
   c) Amalekite military stragglers
   d) the Urim and Thummim

Answers:

1. c (1 Chronicles 21:1–14)
2. wretched (Romans 7:24 kjv)
3. consequences of manipulating God's Word (Proverbs 30:6; Revelation 22:18, Revelation 22:19)
4. the great dragon, that old serpent (kjv)
5. b (1 Samuel 15:13–19)

1. Paul said never to seem
   a) evil.
   b) too friendly to the pagans.
   c) unwilling to share.
   d) uncool.

2. What did the apostle Paul warn the Thessalonians against quenching—or putting out its fire?

3. Connect the Thots:
   the fourth commandment
   the seventh day
   rest

4. What two *L* words complete this scripture from Psalms?
   Your word is a _____ to my feet and a _____ for my path.

5. Evil is to be overcome by
   a) evil.
   b) cutting others down.
   c) the sword.
   d) good.

Answers:

1. a (1 Thessalonians 5:22)
2. the Spirit (1 Thessalonians 5:19)
3. the Sabbath (Exodus 20:3–11)
4. lamp, light (Psalm 119:105 NIV)
5. d (Romans 12:21)

1. What kind of plants and trees did God tell Adam and Eve they could use for food?

2. Complete the scripture:
   I am not ashamed of the gospel of Christ: for it is the _____ of God unto salvation to every one that believeth.

3. What, according to the Song of Solomon, cannot quench love?

4. Connect the Thots:
   Paul, at Cenchrea
   Absalom, when it became too heavy
   Samson, by way of Delilah

5. Match: Mandrake plants. . .
   a) Jacob's favorite food
   b) what Leah gave Rachel in return for Jacob
   c) used to make unleavened bread

1. What name did Jesus give to Simon Peter?
   a) Apollos
   b) Cephas
   c) Demas
   d) Festus

2. Who said the following of Jesus? "This child is destined to cause the falling and rising of many in Israel."

3. Connect the Thots:
   a man journeying to a far country
   five, two, and one
   "Well done, thou good and faithful servant"

4. Jesus said, "I am the good" what?
   a) beekeeper
   b) shepherd
   c) fisherman
   d) camel driver

5. *Jesus* is the Greek form of what Hebrew name that means "the Lord saves"?

Answers:

5. Joshua
4. b (John 10:14)
3. Jesus' parable of the talents (Matthew 25:14–30 KJV)
2. Simeon, upon seeing Jesus as a baby (Luke 2:34 NIV)
1. b (John 1:42)

1. What Israelite, as a powerful official in Egypt, forgave his brothers who years before had sold him into slavery?

2. Whose foolish advice, "Curse God and die," did the righteous, suffering Job resist?
   a) Bildad's
   b) Eliphaz's
   c) Zophar's
   d) his wife's

3. What Old Testament prophet healed the waters of Jericho by throwing salt into a spring?

4. Connect the Thots:
   Evil-Merodach
   Cyrus
   Nebuchadnezzar

5. Match: Terah. . .
   a) He was the grandfather of Lot.
   b) He was the grandfather of Haran.
   c) He was the grandfather of Nahor.

1. The stone on the door of Jesus' tomb was rolled back by
   a) Judas.
   b) Mary Magdalene.
   c) Pharaoh.
   d) an angel.

2. True or False: When Goliath challenged the Israelites to send a man to fight him, many men eagerly volunteered.

3. According to the Proverbs, what is worthless "in the day of wrath"?
   a) power
   b) wealth
   c) fame
   d) idols

4. Connect the Thots:
   the serpent of Revelation
   the wise and foolish builders
   Noah

5. Match: Jesus' resurrection and defeat of Satan. . .
   a) promised first in Genesis
   b) promised first in Exodus
   c) promised first in Psalms

1. What name did God give His Son that "is above every name," according to Paul?

2. According to Micah, where does God place forgiven sins?
   a) beyond the stars
   b) the pit of hell
   c) the depths of the sea
   d) gloomy dungeons

3. What does 1 Corinthians 2:12 say that the Holy Spirit is not the spirit of?

4. True or False: God said that some of Abraham's descendants would be kings.

5. What does God mean when He says not to take His name "in vain"?

Quiz
158

1. What job was held by a Simon from Joppa, who entertained the apostle Peter in his house by the sea?

2. What disciple of Jesus apparently had to overcome a negative disposition—as expressed at the death of Lazarus and the resurrection of Christ?
   a) Matthew
   b) Thomas
   c) Bartholomew
   d) Andrew

3. What new father made this statement: "He has raised up a horn of salvation for us in the house of his servant David"?

4. Connect the Thots:
   the village of Bethany
   sickness and death
   resurrection

5. What did the name "Barnabas" mean?

Answers:

5. Son of encouragement (Acts 4:36 NIV)

4. Lazarus (John 11:1-44)

3. Zechariah, father of John the Baptist (Luke 1:59-60, 67-69 NIV)

2. b (John 11:14-16; 20:24-25)

1. tanner (Acts 10:32-33)

1. What city was the birthplace of the apostle Paul?

2. Match: Bethany. . .
   a) where Jesus ascended to heaven
   b) where Jesus fed the five thousand
   c) where Jesus told His disciples to find a donkey tied there

3. In what city was a paralyzed man lowered through a roof to see Jesus?

4. What more familiar name now applies to the ancient city of Jebus?

5. According to the writer of the book of Acts, how far was it from the Mount of Olives to Jerusalem?

1. What two words complete Jesus' statement "I am the bread..."?

2. Connect the Thots:
   King of the Jews
   the house and lineage of David
   swaddling clothes

3. Filled with compassion, Jesus performed what miracle during the funeral procession for the widow's son?

4. What is Jesus' last statement in the Bible?
   a) "Continue in my love."
   b) "Remember the Lord your God."
   c) "I am coming soon."
   d) "My Father's house awaits you."

5. What two groups motivated Jesus to say, "They be blind leaders of the blind"?

Answers:

5. Pharisees and scribes (Matthew 15:1, 14 KJV)

4. c (Revelation 22:20 NIV)

3. He brought him back to life (Luke 7:14–15)

2. the birth of Jesus (Matthew 2:2; Luke 2:4–5; Luke 2:7)

1. of life (John 6:35)

1. All the silver, gold, bronze, and iron in Jericho was
   a) used to improve the ark of the covenant.
   b) put into the Lord's treasury.
   c) used to build the Tower of Babel.
   d) made into fancy jewelry.

2. What leader of Israel had a staff, or rod, that turned into a snake?

3. Connect the Thots:
   camel
   vulture
   pig

4. What fishing tool did Jesus liken to the kingdom of heaven in a parable found only in Matthew's Gospel?

5. Match: Manna...
   a) twice a day, seven days a week
   b) once a day, six days a week
   c) once a day, seven days a week

1. Match: Adam and Eve...
   a) Adam made garments for Eve and himself.
   b) God made garments for them.
   c) Eve made garments out of animal skins.

2. What sin against the Holy Spirit, according to Jesus, would result in eternal guilt?

3. According to the apostle Paul, the wages of sin is what?
   a) disease
   b) pain
   c) death
   d) grief

4. Complete the scripture:
   "In your anger do not sin": Do not let the _____
   _____ _____ while you are still angry.

5. We shouldn't be jealous of wicked people, because they
   a) will have no reward.
   b) will be cursed.
   c) know the Lord.
   d) will gain weight from eating too much rich food.

Answers:

5. a (Proverbs 24:19–20 kjv)
4. sun go down (Ephesians 4:26 niv)
3. c (Romans 6:23)
2. blasphemy (Mark 3:28–29)
1. b (Genesis 3:21)

1. According to the Proverbs, a good name is what?
   a) better than great riches
   b) difficult to maintain
   c) the heritage of the Lord's children
   d) its own reward

2. What did Jesus tell His disciples to do to the people who cursed them?

3. Complete the scripture:
   Pride goeth before destruction, and an _____ spirit before a fall.

4. What, according to Hebrews, is the Word of God sharper than?
   a) a spear
   b) a flint
   c) a twoedged sword
   d) a thorn

5. What did Jesus promise God the Father would give to anyone who asked?

Answers:

1. a (Proverbs 22:1)
2. bless them (Luke 6:20, 28)
3. haughty (Proverbs 16:18 kjv)
4. c (Hebrews 4:12 kjv)
5. the Holy Spirit (Luke 11:11–13)

• • • • • • • • • • • •

1. Whom did Eve say "replaced" the murdered Abel?
   a) Seth
   b) Enosh
   c) Lamech
   d) Jared

2. How many languages appeared on the sign—reading
   JESUS OF NAZARETH THE KING OF THE JEWS—that
   hung on Jesus' cross?

3. Connect the Thots:
   the darts of the wicked
   the Christian's trials
   Nebuchadnezzar's furnace

4. Match: One hundred...
   a) in talents, what Sheba gave Solomon in gold
   b) in silver pieces, what Jacob paid for land in Canaan
   c) people killed by Samson at Lehi

5. The book of Ezra opens with
   a) Christ's birth.
   b) the end of the Jews' captivity in Babylon.
   c) a psalm of David.
   d) a prophecy about the end of the world.

Answers:

5. b
4. b (Genesis 33:18–19 NIV)
3. fiery things (Ephesians 6:16; 1 Peter 4:12; Daniel 3:19–20)
2. three (John 19:19–20)
1. a (Genesis 4:25)

1. Although Jesus asked the woman at the well for water to drink, what kind of water did He offer to give her?

2. Match: Jesus. . .
   a) promised that the greatest on earth would be greatest in heaven.
   b) promised the Pharisees long life.
   c) promised disciples would one day sit on twelve thrones.

3. Isaiah prophesied that Jesus would be "a man of" what?
   a) joy
   b) sorrows
   c) power
   d) pain

4. Connect the Thots:
   "Man shall not live by bread alone, but by every word of God."
   "Thou shalt worship the Lord thy God, and him only shalt thou serve."
   "Thou shalt not tempt the Lord thy God."

5. When Jesus was on earth, on what two occasions did God speak directly from heaven?

• • • • • • • • • • • •

1. What twin brother of Jacob was born hairy?

2. After he was grown, Moses fled Egypt because he
    a) stole from the treasury.
    b) was found to be a Hebrew.
    c) killed an Egyptian for smiting a Hebrew.
    d) killed a Hebrew for smiting a member of the royal court.

3. Connect the Thots:
    a woman named Zipporah
    a forty-year journey
    tablets of stone

4. Match: Aaron and Moses. . .
    a) Aaron had a speech impediment, so Moses talked to Pharaoh.
    b) Moses created a golden calf from the Hebrews' gold.
    c) Aaron's staff became a snake.

5. When God promised Abraham that his wife Sarah would have a baby, he
    a) praised God.
    b) invested in a college fund.
    c) bought a box of expensive cigars.
    d) laughed.

Answers:

5. d (Genesis 17:16–17)
4. c (Exodus 7:10)
3. Moses (Exodus 2:21; Numbers 14:26–34; Exodus 31:18)
2. c (Exodus 2:11–12, 15)
1. Esau (Genesis 25:25–26)

1. What hostile army, pursuing the people of Israel, was completely destroyed in the middle of the Red Sea?

2. Connect the Thots:
    an ax head that floated
    bears that mauled mouthy kids
    a Shunammite boy raised from the dead

3. Match: The plague of blood. . .
    a) Egypt's magicians were unable to change water into blood.
    b) Aaron struck the Nile with his staff.
    c) Despite the plague, Egyptians could still drink the water.

4. What was Euroclydon?

5. What did the people of Malta say about Paul when a snakebite didn't kill him?
    a) that he was lucky
    b) that he was a demon
    c) that he was a god
    d) that he was really tough

• • • • • • • • • •

1. When God spoke to Moses, what name did the Lord use for Himself?

2. The Holy Spirit bears witness with us that we are what to God?

3. When did it happen that "God created the heavens and the earth"?
   a) Billions of years ago. . .
   b) In the fullness of time. . .
   c) In the beginning. . .
   d) From ancient times. . .

4. In addition to one body, one Spirit, one hope, one Lord, one faith, and one baptism, what else does Ephesians say we have one of?

5. The statement "For nothing is impossible with God" referred to what miracle?
   a) salvation for the Gentiles
   b) raising the dead
   c) the virgin birth of Jesus
   d) Elizabeth becoming a mother

Answers:

5. d (Luke 1:36–37)
4. one God and Father (Ephesians 4:4–6)
3. c (Genesis 1:1)
2. His children (Romans 8:16)
1. I AM and/or I AM THAT I AM (Exodus 3:14 kjv)

1. What professional title, besides missionary, did Luke hold?

2. Connect the Thots:
   a brother of Jesus
   the Cyrenian who carried Jesus' cross
   a Canaanite disciple

3. Which New Testament writer says we are a holy priesthood, a royal priesthood?

4. Match: Rhoda...
   a) daughter of Herodias who danced at Herod's birthday
   b) sister of Laban
   c) servant who recognized Peter's voice

5. What devout Gentile received a visit from the angel of the Lord?

Answers:

5. Cornelius (Acts 10:1–3)
4. c (Acts 12:13–14)
3. Peter (1 Peter 2:5, 9)
2. men named Simon (Matthew 13:55; Matthew 27:32; Matthew 10:2–4)
1. doctor (Colossians 4:14)

• • • • • • • • • • • •

1. What town was home to Jesse's boys?

2. Match: Athens. . .
   a) where Paul spent his boyhood
   b) where Jason's house was located
   c) where Paul spoke of an idol to an unknown god

3. Where will the Lord live when he returns to earth?

4. King Ahab wanted the vineyard of Naboth the Jezreelite because
   a) it was near his palace and he wanted to use it as a vegetable garden.
   b) it was a perfect location to film his latest movie.
   c) he needed the land so he could build a temple to Baal.
   d) his goats needed more land for pasture.

5. Who alone could enter the Holy of Holies and on what occasion?

Answers:

5. the high priest on the Day of Atonement (Leviticus 16)
4. a (1 Kings 21:2)
3. Zion (Joel 3:21)
2. c (Acts 17:22–23)
1. Bethlehem (1 Samuel 17:58)

1. Which of the following baking items did Jesus compare to the kingdom of heaven?
    a) a pan
    b) flour
    c) an egg
    d) yeast

2. Connect the Thots:
    water turned into wine
    a storm calmed
    ten lepers cleansed

3. What word is the Greek equivalent of *Messiah*?

4. Matthew says that the criminals crucified with Christ were
    a) murderers.
    b) tax collectors.
    c) thieves.
    d) all of the above.

5. Match: Immanuel. . .
    a) Jesus
    b) Isaiah
    c) Jeremiah

Answers:

1. d (Matthew 13:33 niv)
2. miracles of Jesus (John 2:1–11; Matthew 8:23–27; Luke 17:11–19)
3. Christ
4. c (Matthew 27:44 kjv)
5. a (Matthew 1:23 niv)

1. What two animals represent the saved and lost people of earth, whom Jesus will separate at the final judgment?

2. Connect the Thots:
   Samson's snack of honey
   David's dangerous shepherd duty
   Jesus' title "of the tribe of Judah"

3. According to God, of what kind of wood was the ark to be made?

4. Match: Tabernacle bread. . .
   a) seven loaves
   b) ten loaves
   c) twelve loaves

5. What was engraved on the front of the high priest's turban?

Answers:

5. a gold plate was engraved with HOLINESS TO THE LORD (Exodus 28:36–38 kjv)

4. c (Leviticus 24:3–5)

3. Gopher wood (Genesis 6:14 kjv)

2. lions (Judges 14:5–9; 1 Samuel 17:34–36; Revelation 5:5)

1. sheep and goats (Matthew 25:31–33)

1. According to the Proverbs, a prostitute reduces a man to what?
    a) a brute beast
    b) a blind beggar
    c) a blemished bull
    d) a bite of bread

2. What "lake" is the final, eternal home for those people whose names are not found in the book of life?

3. Connect the Thots:
    Abimelech's demise
    forbidden as pledge for a debt
    punishment for causing a child to sin

4. What happened to the prophet who ate and drank when God told him not to?

5. What was the apostle Paul's rule toward people who refused to work?
    a) They should be prayed over.
    b) They should not eat.
    c) They should be disciplined by the church.
    d) They should not expect charity.

Answers:

5. b (2 Thessalonians 3:10)
4. A lion killed him (1 Kings 13:20–24).
3. millstones (Judges 9:52–53; Deuteronomy 24:6; Matthew 18:6)
2. the lake of fire (Revelation 20:15)
1. d (Proverbs 6:20, 26 kjv)

1. John says that when someone pretends to be a Christian but really isn't, you should
   a) not let the person into your house.
   b) pretend you don't speak English.
   c) spread the blood of a lamb on your door.
   d) tell everybody you know.

2. What, along with godliness, did the apostle Paul tell Timothy "is great gain"?

3. Jesus says He will give His believers what two *W* words when we are brought before our adversaries on account of His name?

4. Throughout his first letter, John tells Christians not to love
   a) their brothers.
   b) pagans.
   c) television.
   d) the world.

5. If we show love only to those who love us, we are no better than whom?

Answers:

1. a (2 John 1:7–10)
2. contentment (1 Timothy 6:6 niv)
3. words and wisdom (Luke 21:15 niv)
4. d (1 John 2:15)
5. Jesus says we are no better than the publicans, or tax collectors, some of the most hated people of His time (Matthew 5:46–47).

1. What did the Philistines, envious of Isaac's wealth in flocks and herds, try to destroy?

2. Connect the Thots:
   merry
   deceitful
   hardened

3. Whose name means "morning star" or "son of the morning"?

4. Match: Fifty-two...
   a) days Nehemiah spent rebuilding Jerusalem's wall
   b) days Jesus fasted in the wilderness
   c) messengers Jesus sent out as missionaries

5. What kind of tree caught Absalom's head as he rode underneath on a mule, leaving him hanging?

Answers:

1. wells (Genesis 26:12–15)
2. kinds of hearts (Proverbs 17:22 kjv; Jeremiah 17:9; Exodus 7:14 kjv)
3. Lucifer (Isaiah 14:12)
4. a (Nehemiah 2:17; 6:15)
5. oak (2 Samuel 18:9–10)

1. How many years, according to John's Revelation, will Jesus reign on earth before Satan's final judgment?

2. Connect the Thots:
   Word of God
   Lamb of God
   Son of God

3. Why was Jesus in Jerusalem when he got separated from His parents?

4. How long did Jesus' parents search before they found Him?

5. How many siblings, the natural children of Mary and Joseph, did Jesus have?
   a) none
   b) two
   c) four
   d) six or more

1. Abraham's servant gave Rebekah
   a) a Happy Meal.
   b) three sheep.
   c) silver jewelry.
   d) gold jewelry.

2. What woman, the wife of Elkanah, was mother of the prophet Samuel?

3. What prophet went into depression when the evil Queen Jezebel threatened his life?
   a) Isaiah
   b) Nathan
   c) Samuel
   d) Elijah

4. Connect the Thots:
   a young protégé
   wicked sons
   a broken neck

5. Match: Joseph and his brothers. . .
   a) Joseph planted his own silver cup in Benjamin's sack.
   b) Reuben asked to stay in Egypt in place of Benjamin.
   c) Joseph's brothers sold him for thirty shekels to Midianite merchants.

Answers:

5. a (Genesis 44:1–2, 12)
4. Eli the priest (1 Samuel 2:11–12; 1 Samuel 4:16–18)
3. d (1 Kings 19:1–4)
2. Hannah (1 Samuel 1:19–20)
1. d (Genesis 24:1–2, 10–22)

1. True or False: Mary and Joseph had been married for twenty years before she became pregnant by the Holy Spirit.

2. To divide the Red Sea, Moses lifted
   a) the belt of his robe.
   b) both hands.
   c) the name of the Lord.
   d) his hand and his rod.

3. Connect the Thots:
   a centurion named Julius
   Euroclydon
   a shipwreck

4. True or False: Elisha told the kings to build ditches in a dry streambed.

5. What young king removed all the mediums and spiritists from Judah, as required in the Book of the Law found by his priest, Hilkiah?

Answers:

5. Josiah (2 Kings 22:1–8; 23:24–25)
4. True (2 Kings 3:13–16)
3. the apostle Paul's journey to Rome (Acts 27:1–44)
2. d (Exodus 14:15–16, 21)
1. False

1. When Jesus said He is the "true vine," who did He say is the gardener?

2. What famous Bible personality did God name "Jedidiah"?
   a) Noah
   b) Solomon
   c) Jeremiah
   d) Daniel

3. What does God say in Genesis 6:3 (KJV) that His Spirit will not always do?

4. True or False: As part of His covenant with Abraham, God wanted Abraham and his descendants to worship Him.

5. God tells us to honor our
   a) pastor.
   b) friends.
   c) father and mother.
   d) teachers and principal.

Answers:

5. c (Exodus 20:12; Deuteronomy 5:16)
4. True (Genesis 17:7)
3. strive with men
2. b (2 Samuel 12:24–25)
1. His Father (John 15:1)

Quiz
180

• • • • • • • • • • • •

1. What servant of the high priest had his ear sliced off by Peter's sword—then restored by Jesus—during Jesus' arrest?

2. Connect the Thots:
   Ananias
   Caiaphas
   Jesus Christ

3. What high priest did Paul call a whitewashed wall?

4. Match: Phoebe...
   a) wife of Felix
   b) servant or deaconess of the early church
   c) wife of Herod Agrippa

5. Which disciple brought the boy with the five loaves and two fish to Jesus?

Answers:

1. Malchus (Luke 22:50–51; John 18:10)
2. high priests (Acts 23:2; John 18:13; Hebrews 3:1)
3. Ananias (Acts 23:2–3 NIV)
4. b (Romans 16:1)
5. Andrew (John 6:8–9)

1. What wicked city did Jesus pair with Sodom?

2. Connect the Thots:
   Pergamos
   Sardis
   Philadelphia

3. What town, along with Bethsaida, did not repent when Jesus performed miracles there and thus received a pronouncement of woe?

4. Match: Valley of Sorek. . .
   a) where Samuel anointed David
   b) where Samson fell in love with Delilah
   c) where Ruth fell in love with Boaz

5. The book of Nahum prophesies the fall of what city?
   a) Babylon
   b) Tyre
   c) Susa
   d) Nineveh

1. To whom did Jesus say, "Every. . .house divided against itself shall not stand"?

2. Match: Wonderful Counselor. . .
   a) first used by Jeremiah
   b) first used by Isaiah
   c) first used in the Psalms by David

3. How many criminals were crucified with Jesus at Golgotha?

4. Connect the Thots:
   midday darkness
   a centurion praising God
   "Into thy hands I commend my spirit"

5. Who are the four women mentioned in Jesus' genealogy in Matthew 1 (NIV)?

1. What type of tree does the love-smitten woman of the Song of Solomon compare her man to?

2. What metal, used to sharpen other like metal, does Proverbs compare to friends?

3. Connect the Thots:
   Amos's vision of a basket
   love, joy, peace, etc.
   the tree of the knowledge of good and evil

4. What herbs did Jesus say the Pharisees tithed?

5. What part of a dead donkey did Samson use to kill one thousand enemy Philistines?

• • • • • • • • • • •

1. Who was stoned to death after admitting he had stolen clothing, silver, and gold from the ruins of Jericho?

2. The unrepentant criminal who was crucified with Jesus asked Him to
   a) turn stones into bread.
   b) ask a centurion for a cup of water.
   c) bless him and his family.
   d) save Himself and them.

3. In asking for this, the unrepentant criminal was asking Jesus to prove what?

4. Connect the Thots:
   a proud look
   a lying tongue
   hands that shed innocent blood

5. What prophet got so angry at God that he told God to just go ahead and kill him?

Answers:

5. Jonah (Jonah 4:1–3)

4. things the Lord hates (Proverbs 6:16–19)

3. that he is the Christ (Luke 23:39)

2. d (Luke 23:39)

1. Achan (Joshua 7:19–25)

1. What piece of the armor of God can quench the fiery darts or flaming arrows of Satan?

2. John says that true Christians have
   a) love.
   b) fear.
   c) gold plaques with their names engraved on them.
   d) money invested in John's real estate firm.

3. What does Jesus say the angels do when one sinner repents?

4. True or False: We don't have to forgive anybody who doesn't ask us for forgiveness.

5. When Jesus speaks of neighbors, He means
   a) the people who live in the house next to yours.
   b) everyone.
   c) the people who live in your town.
   d) your enemies.

Answers:

1. the shield of faith (Ephesians 6:16 kjv)
2. a (1 John 2:5)
3. they rejoice; there is joy (Luke 15:10)
4. False (Luke 6:37)
5. b

1. What musical instrument accompanies the song of victorious saints in heaven, according to John's Revelation?

2. Connect the Thots:
   Saul on the road to Damascus
   men of Sodom, at Lot's house
   Bartimaeus

3. What would King Xerxes hold out to show favor to the people who pleased him?

4. Match: Fourteen...
   a) generations from Babylonian exile to birth of Jesus
   b) days Jesus was tempted by Satan in the desert
   c) months Paul spent on Malta

5. Who killed two people at once with one spear?

1. How did the soldiers at Golgotha decide who should receive Jesus' clothing?

2. Connect the Thots:
   Matthat
   Heli
   Joseph

3. When the disciples asked Jesus to tell them the signs of His coming and the end of the age, what prophet did Jesus quote?

4. Complete the scripture:
   God made him who had no _____ to be _____ for us, so that in him we might become the righteousness of God.

5. Match: How Jesus became the Nazarene...
   a) Joseph was told to go to Nazareth in a dream.
   b) Simeon told Joseph to go to Nazareth.
   c) Zechariah told Joseph to go to Nazareth.

Answers:

5. a (Matthew 2:19–23)

4. sin, sin (2 Corinthians 5:21 NIV)

3. Daniel (Matthew 24:3, 15)

2. the family line of Jesus (Luke 3:23–24)

1. by casting lots (John 19:23–24)

1. What Bible strongman lost his power when his long hair was cut off?

2. What Old Testament leader overcame a huge enemy army, "like grasshoppers for multitude," with three hundred men handpicked by God Himself?
   a) Samson
   b) Gideon
   c) David
   d) Saul

3. What judge of Israel made a foolish vow that cost him the life of his only daughter?

4. Connect the Thots:
   Elijah
   Haggai
   Daniel

5. Match: Cain and Abel. . .
   a) Abel worked the soil while Cain tended the sheep.
   b) Abel was sentenced by God to wander the earth.
   c) Cain was sent to live east of Eden.

Answers:

5. c (Genesis 4:16)
4. prophets (1 Kings 18:36; Haggai 2:1; Matthew 24:15)
3. Jephthah (Judges 11:30–39)
2. b (Judges 7:1–25 kjv)
1. Samson (Judges 16:15–20)

1. After Goliath died, the Israelites
    a) chased the Philistines back to their own country.
    b) offered the Philistines a permanent peace treaty.
    c) slept.
    d) sang "I'm in the Lord's Army!"

2. What event in Jesus' life featured a voice from heaven saying, "This is my Son, whom I love"?

3. Connect the Thots:
    an abundance of frogs
    three days of darkness
    the death of firstborn sons

4. Complete the scripture:
    "Take off your sandals, for the place you are standing is
    _____ _____."

5. The Feast of Tabernacles commemorated
    a) Jesus' birth in a stable.
    b) the building of Solomon's temple.
    c) the forty years' wandering in the wilderness.
    d) the Mormon Tabernacle Choir.

Answers:

1. a (1 Samuel 17:4, 51–52)
2. His baptism (Matthew 3:16–17 NIV)
3. plagues on Egypt (Exodus 8:3; Exodus 10:21–22; Exodus 11:5)
4. holy, ground (Exodus 3:5)
5. c (Leviticus 23:33–43)

1. To whom did Jesus say, "My Father is always at his work to this very day, and I, too, am working"?

2. Which of the following does the Bible say God keeps numbered?
   a) the hairs of your head
   b) the trees of the forest
   c) the fish of the sea
   d) the burgers served at McDonald's

3. What are five symbols of the Holy Spirit?

4. God tells us not to covet other people's possessions. That means we should not
   a) steal from our friends.
   b) destroy other people's belongings.
   c) make fun of others.
   d) wish we had our neighbor's stuff.

5. What fourteen-letter word defined the ministry that Paul told the Corinthians God has given those who are in Christ?

Answers:

5. reconciliation (2 Corinthians 5:18)

4. d

3. water (John 7:38–39), wind or Spirit (John 3:8), seal (Ephesians 1:13), dove (Matthew 3:16), fire (Acts 2:3–4)

2. a (Matthew 10:30)

1. the Jews at the temple (John 5:16–17 NIV)

1. What wicked New Testament king "was eaten by worms and died" for allowing people to call him a god?

2. Connect the Thots:
   Aristarchus
   Tychicus
   Aquila and Priscilla

3. What mother-to-be made this statement? "My soul glorifies the Lord and my spirit rejoices in God my Savior."

4. How many descriptions are given of Judas Iscariot's death?

5. What was Pontius Pilate's job?

Answers:

1. Herod (Acts 12:21–23 niv)
2. coworkers with the apostle Paul (Colossians 4:10; Colossians 4:7; Romans 16:3)
3. Mary (Luke 1:30–33, 46–47 niv)
4. two (Matthew 27:5; Acts 1:18)
5. governor of Judea (Luke 3:1)

1. What sea was the location of Jesus' calling of Peter and Andrew?

2. Match: Bethel. . .
    a) where Lazarus lived
    b) where a pool existed known for its healing powers
    c) where Jacob built an altar

3. Where did Paul meet Aquila and Priscilla?

4. Naboth refused to let King Ahab have his vineyard because
    a) he had lost the deed to the land in a Monopoly game.
    b) the land belonged to his mother-in-law.
    c) the land was not good enough for the glorious King Ahab.
    d) God refused to let him give King Ahab the land.

5. What separated the Holy Place from the Most Holy Place?

1. From what mountain did Jesus talk about the end times?

2. Complete Jesus' sentence: "The Son of Man did not come to be served, but to serve, and to give his life as a _____ for many."

3. What "amazed" Jesus about the people of His hometown?

4. Connect the Thots:
   "The Son of man hath not where to lay his head."
   "Let the dead bury their dead."
   "No man, having put his hand to the plough, and looking back, is fit for the kingdom of God."

5. Whom does the author of Hebrews trust?

1. What kind of animal was the "prodigal son" feeding when he realized he should return home to his father?

2. Connect the Thots:
   wild goat
   leviathan
   behemoth

3. Match: Eagle feathers. . .
   a) what Nebuchadnezzar wore in his crown
   b) what Nebuchadnezzar's hair looked like, to fulfill his dream
   c) what Nebuchadnezzar collected

4. What gem "of great value" did Jesus mention in a parable found only in Matthew's Gospel?

5. What was the "forbidden fruit" that Adam and Eve ate?
   a) an apple
   b) a fig
   c) a pear
   d) it's not specified

Answers:

5. d (Genesis 3:6)
4. pearl (Matthew 13:45–46 NIV)
3. b (Daniel 4:33)
2. creatures in the book of Job (Job 39:1 KJV; Job 41:1; Job 40:15)
1. pigs (Luke 15:11–20)

1. What Old Testament prophet had to buy back his adulterous wife with silver and barley?

2. What was the name of the above-mentioned prophet's wife?
   a) Abigail
   b) Gomer
   c) Tamar
   d) Tryphena

3. What punishment did God give humankind because their every thought was "evil continually"?

4. Connect the Thots:
   fornicators
   idolators
   thieves

5. According to the Proverbs, what is true of an adulterous woman's speech?
   a) It is smoother than oil.
   b) It has ensnared many young men.
   c) It is full of lies.
   d) It can confuse the wise.

Answers:

5. a (Proverbs 5:3)

4. people who won't inherit the kingdom of God (1 Corinthians 6:9–10 kjv)

3. the flood (Genesis 6 kjv)

2. b (Hosea 1:3)

1. Hosea (Hosea 3:1–2)

1. What troublesome desire did Paul say is "common to man"?

2. Connect the Thots:
   a house built on rock
   new wine in old bottles
   an unmerciful servant

3. No branch can bear fruit unless it does what?

4. Regarding enemies, Jesus said we are to
   a) love them.
   b) bless them.
   c) pray for them.
   d) all of the above.

5. According to Jesus, people will know we are His disciples when we
   a) get three perfect attendance pins at church.
   b) love one another.
   c) go to vacation Bible school every year.
   d) listen to Christian radio stations every day.

Answers:

1. temptation (1 Corinthians 10:13 NIV)
2. parables of Jesus (Matthew 7:24–27; Mark 2:19–22; Matthew 18:21–35)
3. remain in the Vine (John 15:4)
4. d (Matthew 5:43–44 KJV)
5. b (John 13:34–35)

1. What kind of cakes did Abigail take to King David to apologize for her husband's rude behavior?

2. Connect the Thots:
   the selection of Matthias as an apostle
   soldiers competing for the crucified Jesus' clothing
   Jonah determined as the cause of a storm at sea

3. Match: Seven. . .
   a) banquets Esther hosted for Haman and Xerxes
   b) times Shunammite's son sneezed after Elisha restored his life
   c) coins widow deposited in temple treasury

4. True or False: Both criminals who were crucified with Jesus thought He was guilty of the crimes with which He was charged.

5. According to the Proverbs, "a good name is" what?
   a) better than great riches
   b) difficult to maintain
   c) the heritage of the Lord's children
   d) its own reward

• • • • • • • • • • •

1. What did mocking soldiers offer Jesus to drink while He hung on the cross at Golgotha?

2. Connect the Thots:
   go into all the world
   teach all nations
   baptize

3. When the chief priests and elders demanded to know by what authority Jesus taught, what question did Jesus use to confound them?

4. According to the apostle John, "Everyone who believes that Jesus is the Messiah is born of _____."

5. Paul writes to the Romans, "The night is nearly over; the day is almost here." What does he mean by "the day"?

1. Joseph's father loved him more than any of his other children because Joseph
    a) was the child of his old age.
    b) was handsome.
    c) had good taste in clothes.
    d) showered him with gold, frankincense, and myrrh.

2. What man lived the longest life recorded in the Bible—969 years?

3. When Miriam is first mentioned by name in the Bible, she is
    a) drinking wine.
    b) celebrating the Israelites' victory over the Canaanites.
    c) leading the women in song and dance.
    d) predicting good tidings for Israel.

4. Connect the Thots:
    shepherd
    harpist
    king

5. Match: Absalom, Amnon, and Tamar. . .
    a) Amnon fell in love with his half sister Tamar.
    b) Absalom banished Amnon from Israel.
    c) Absalom killed himself out of shame for his sister.

Answers:

5. a (2 Samuel 13:1)
4. David (1 Samuel 16:11–13; 1 Samuel 16:23; 2 Samuel 2:4)
3. c (Exodus 15:20)
2. Methuselah (Genesis 5:27)
1. a (Genesis 37:3)

1. What miracle occurred in the heavens the day Joshua and the Israelites defeated the armies of the Amorites?

2. When Mary Magdalene first saw the empty tomb, she
   a) rejoiced.
   b) was angry.
   c) questioned the guards.
   d) wept.

3. True or False: Elisha purified a pot of stew that contained poisonous gourds.

4. Connect the Thots:
   a donkey and a colt
   clothes and branches on the roadway
   people shouting, "Hosanna!"

5. Why did David visit the Israelites' battlefield?

Answers:

1. the sun stood still (Joshua 10:9–14)
2. d (John 20:1, 11)
3. True (2 Kings 4:38–41)
4. Jesus' triumphal entry into Jerusalem (Matthew 21:1–11)
5. David was taking food to his three older brothers who were soldiers in battle (1 Samuel 17:13, 17–18)

1. What protective structures, which proved inadequate for Jericho, did God warn Israel against trusting in?

2. True or False: When you pray, you should always give thanks to God.

3. According to the prophet Joel, what would the Holy Spirit enable young men and young women to do?

4. According the apostle Paul, the Christian's body is the what of the Holy Spirit?
   a) temple
   b) house
   c) chariot
   d) slave

5. What two words describe the throne on which God sits while passing final judgment on those who have died?

1. What New Testament preacher, like the Old Testament hero Samson, was never to drink wine or other fermented drink?

2. What two disciples from Jesus' inner circle, described as "unschooled, ordinary men," amazed the Jewish leaders with their courage in preaching the gospel?

3. Connect the Thots:
   husband Zechariah
   son John
   cousin Mary

4. What was the occupation of the Ethiopian eunuch in Acts 8?

5. What two groups of philosophers questioned Paul in Athens?

Answers:

5. Epicureans and Stoics (Acts 17:18 NIV)
4. treasurer (Acts 8:27)
3. Elizabeth (Luke 1:5 NIV; Luke 1:57–60 NIV; Luke 1:34–37 NIV)
2. Peter and John (Acts 4:1–20)
1. John the Baptist (Judges 13:5, 24; Luke 1:13–15)

1. What kind of place was Patmos, where John received his Revelation of Jesus Christ?

2. Connect the Thots:
   Achor
   Hinnom
   the shadow of death

3. What river connects the Sea of Galilee with the Dead Sea?

4. Match: Cenchrea...
   a) where Ur was located
   b) where Paul shaved his head
   c) region named after Caesar Augustus

5. Where did Abraham find a ram to sacrifice after God stopped him from sacrificing his son Isaac?

Answers:

5. thicket (Genesis 22:9–13)
4. b (Acts 18:18)
3. the Jordan River
2. valleys (Joshua 7:26; Joshua 18:16; Psalm 23:4)
1. island (Revelation 1:9)

Quiz
204

1. Connect the Thots:
   a napkin
   linen cloths
   an empty tomb

2. What religious group did Jesus twice call a "brood (or generation) of vipers"?

3. Who wove the crown of thorns that Jesus wore?
   a) Pontius Pilate
   b) Caiaphas, the high priest
   c) Herod
   d) Roman soldiers

4. While Jesus had given the disciples authority to perform miracles in His name, what did He want them to rejoice about instead?

5. Match: Jesus' clearing of the temple. . .
   a) on the same day as the triumphal entry
   b) on the same day as the Olivet Discourse
   c) on the day after the triumphal entry

Answers:

1. the resurrection of Jesus (John 20:1–9 kjv)
2. the Pharisees (Matthew 12:24–34; 23:29–33)
3. d (John 19:2)
4. that their names were written in heaven (Luke 10:19–20)
5. c (Mark 11:1–17)

1. What was Saul looking for when he learned he would become the king of Israel?
   a) a wife
   b) lost donkeys
   c) water
   d) a job

2. What insect made a large part of the diet of John the Baptist?

3. Connect the Thots:
   corruptible versus incorruptible
   Jesus' thorns
   cast before God's throne

4. What two animals did David boast of killing?

5. Which of the following is not a food the Israelites craved from Egypt?
   a) cucumbers
   b) melons
   c) onions
   d) apples

5. d (Numbers 11:5)
4. bear, lion (1 Samuel 17:34–36)
3. crowns (1 Corinthians 9:25; John 19:5; Revelation 4:10–11)
2. locusts (Matthew 3:4)
1. b (1 Samuel 10:1–2)

Quiz
206

1. What sin was a woman caught in by scribes and Pharisees who then tried to trick Jesus into approving her death by stoning?

2. True or False: The Lord called Aaron and Miriam into the tabernacle to chasten them for speaking against Moses.

3. What were Barabbas's crimes?

4. What group of people, according to the apostle Paul, might "learn to be idle" and turn away from God?
   a) young widows
   b) the rich
   c) old men
   d) children

5. Complete the scripture:
   Jesus says of the man who betrayed the Son of Man, "It would be better for him if __ __ __ ___ ___."

Answers:

5. he had not been born (Matthew 26:24 niv)

4. a (1 Timothy 5:11–15 kjv)

3. robbery (John 18:40), insurrection/sedition, and murder (Mark 15:7; Luke 23:18–19)

2. True (Numbers 12:5–8)

1. adultery (John 8:1–11)

Quiz
207

1. What "visual aid" did Jesus use to answer the disciples' question, "Who is the greatest in the kingdom of heaven?"

2. What two *S* words complete this scripture?
   Take the helmet of _____ and the sword of the
   _____.

3. Complete this quotation of Jesus: "Foxes have holes, and birds of the air have nests, but the Son of Man. . ."
   a) "has a beautiful palace in heaven."
   b) "has a small home in Jerusalem."
   c) "has no place to lay his head."
   d) "has twelve disciples to live with."

4. True or False: The disciples always understood the parables without Jesus having to explain them.

5. What question was Jesus answering when He told the parable of the good Samaritan?

Answers:

5. "And who is my neighbour?" (Luke 10:29–37 kjv)
4. False (Matthew 13:36)
3. c (Matthew 8:20 niv)
2. salvation, Spirit (Ephesians 6:17)
1. a child (Matthew 18:1–4)

1. What did Jesus eat in the presence of His disciples shortly after His resurrection?

2. Connect the Thots:
   Abib
   Adar
   Elul

3. What kind of fire does the prophet Malachi say the Lord will be like in the day of judgment?

4. Match: Deborah. . .
   a) wife of Barak
   b) held court under the Palm of Deborah
   c) sister of Jael, Sisera's slayer

5. What does Ebenezer mean?

Answers:

5. "stone of help" (1 Samuel 7:12)
4. b (Judges 4:4–5)
3. refiner's (Malachi 3:1–2)
2. months of the Hebrew calendar (Exodus 13:4; Esther 3:7; Nehemiah 6:15)
1. broiled fish (Luke 24:36–43)

1. What animal feeding trough served as a temporary bed for the newborn Jesus?

2. What did John the Baptist say he was unworthy of doing for Christ?
   a) bearing His name
   b) untying His sandals
   c) performing His ministry
   d) cooking His supper

3. How did John the Baptist address Jesus when he saw Him by the Jordan?

4. After the Sabbath, what did Salome, Mary Magdalene, and Mary the mother of James take to the tomb of Jesus?
   a) spices
   b) burial linens
   c) olive branches and flowers
   d) marker of stones for His tomb

5. In the middle of a fierce storm, what did Jesus say to the wind and the waves?

Answers:

5. "Quiet! Be still!" (Mark 4:39 NIV)
4. a (Mark 16:1)
3. Lamb of God (John 1:29)
2. b (Luke 3:16)
1. a manger (Luke 2:4–11)

1. What king of Tyre supplied cedar logs to Solomon for building the Lord's temple?

2. How old was Joseph when, after years of false imprisonment, he rose to become second-in-command of Egypt?
   a) Eighteen years old
   b) Thirty years old
   c) Fifty years old
   d) Ninety years old

3. What widowed woman left her mother-in-law, Naomi, and sister-in-law, Ruth, to return to Moab, her homeland?

4. Connect the Thots:
   a priest in Nehemiah's day
   a warrior in David's army
   the weeping prophet

5. Match: Jonathan. . .
   a) He thrust his sword into his father, Saul, as he was dying.
   b) He warned David to flee by shooting arrows.
   c) His disabled son, Mephibosheth, was refused a place at David's table.

Answers:

5. b (1 Samuel 20:35–42)
Jeremiah 13:17)
4. men named Jeremiah (Nehemiah 12:1; 1 Chronicles 12:1–4,
3. Orpah (Ruth 1:3–5, 14–15)
2. b (Genesis 41:14–46)
1. Hiram (1 Kings 5:1–12)

1. When the local people found out that Jesus had driven the mob of demons out of a man, they
   a) feasted for a week.
   b) were afraid.
   c) composed a song in His honor.
   d) made Jesus the town's mayor.

2. Where were the Israelites to apply some of the blood from the Passover sacrifice?

3. Connect the Thots:
   the captain of the host of the Lord
   Joshua
   walking around a city for seven days

4. Who led the victory song after the Egyptians were drowned in the Red Sea?

5. During the Feast of the Tabernacles, native Israelites were instructed to live in
   a) stables.
   b) the temple.
   c) booths.
   d) choir lofts.

1. What was the name of the altar that Moses built after the battle where he had to hold up his hands in order for the army to prevail?

2. Complete the scripture:
   Thy word is a _____ unto my feet.

3. According to Psalm 19, what of the Lord's are true and righteous?

4. True or False: God said to let poor people win lawsuits because they are poor.

5. According to Paul, what will we not fulfill if we walk in the Spirit?

Answers:

5. the lust of the flesh (Galatians 5:16 kjv)
4. False (Exodus 23:2–3)
3. judgments (Psalm 19:9 kjv)
2. lamp (Psalm 119:105 kjv)
1. Jehovah-nissi—The Lord Is My Banner (Exodus 17:10–15)

Quiz
213

1. What imprisoned preacher sent his own disciples to Jesus to ask if He was the expected Messiah?

2. Connect the Thots:
   He lied to the apostles.
   He restored Saul's sight.
   He ordered the apostle Paul struck.

3. What did Zacchaeus do so that he could see Jesus?

4. Match: Herodias. . .
   a) was married to Herod.
   b) had a daughter who was asked to dance on Herod's birthday.
   c) was married to Herod Antipas.

5. In what town did Martha live?

1. What modern-day nation, with its capital at New Delhi, marked the eastern extent of King Xerxes's nation?

2. Connect the Thots:
   Magog
   Babylon
   Armageddon

3. On what mountain is the Garden of Gethsemane located?

4. Match: Zered Valley...
   a) where Moses led the Israelites after thirty-eight years of wandering
   b) where the Israelites defeated the Moabites
   c) where the Israelites defeated the Ammonites

5. What was the name of the valley from which came the word *Gehenna*, or "hell," where children were sacrificed by fire to pagan gods?

Answers:

5. Valley of Hinnom (2 Kings 23:10)

4. a (Deuteronomy 2:13–14 NIV)

3. Mount of Olives

2. places in the book of Revelation (Revelation 20:7–8; Revelation 17:5; Revelation 16:16)

1. India (Esther 8:9)

1. Why did Joseph and Mary take Jesus to Jerusalem when He was twelve years old?

2. To which of the following did Jesus not liken the kingdom of heaven?
   a) a fish net
   b) a wedding banquet
   c) a fire
   d) a hidden treasure

3. In Matthew 5:17, what did Jesus say He came to do to the Law and Prophets?

4. Match: Branch...
   a) so named by Isaiah
   b) so named by Jeremiah
   c) so named by Daniel

5. In what parable did Jesus tell the chief priests and elders that publicans and harlots would enter the kingdom of God before they did?

Answers:

5. the parable of the two sons (Matthew 21:31 kjv)
4. b (Jeremiah 23:5)
3. fulfill them (Matthew 5:17)
2. c (Matthew 13:44, 47; 22:2)
1. to celebrate the Feast of the Passover (Luke 2:41–42)

Quiz
216

• • • • • • • • • • •

1. What insect swarmed Egypt in the fourth plague on Pharaoh—but stayed out of the land of Goshen where God's people lived?

2. Connect the Thots:
   mite
   farthing
   penny

3. When Noah got off the ark, what did he plant?

4. What type of bird does God say Ephraim—the nation of Israel—is like?

5. When God compared Israel to this bird, he meant Israel was
   a) strong and true.
   b) soaring upward.
   c) soft and feathery.
   d) flitting from place to place.

Answers:

5. d (Hosea 7:12)

4. a silly dove (Hosea 7:11–12)

3. a vineyard (Genesis 8:16–18; 9:20)

2. types of money (Mark 12:42 kjv; Luke 12:6 kjv; Matthew 22:19 kjv)

1. flies (Exodus 8:20–24)

1. What does Numbers 32:23 say will happen if you sin?

2. What fellow worker did the apostle Paul say "hath forsaken me, having loved this present world"?
   a) Demas
   b) Tychicus
   c) Luke
   d) Epaphroditus

3. In addition to betraying Jesus, what other crime did Judas Iscariot commit?

4. True or False: Jesus teaches that when people say mean things to you or about you, you should be kind to them anyway.

5. What was the name of the evil spirit that possessed the man who lived in the tombs?

• • • • • • • • • • • •

1. What does the apostle Paul urge Christians to be "...of God"?

2. Complete the scripture:
   If any of you lack _____, let him ask of God. . .and it shall be given him.

3. Where did Jesus teach that we should pray?

4. Connect the Thots:
   Noah found it
   God's is sufficient
   come boldly to the throne of

5. In the four Gospels, we can find
   a) stories Jesus told.
   b) Jesus' family lineage.
   c) accounts of Jesus' resurrection.
   d) all of the above.

1. What part of Jesus' body did a sinful woman anoint with perfume and kiss during a dinner at a Pharisee's house?

2. Connect the Thots:
    baby Moses in his floating basket
    Jesus at Lazarus's tomb
    Peter after denying Christ

3. Match: Seventy. . .
    a) number of Solomon's wives
    b) number of half brothers of Abimelech
    c) number of Solomon's concubines

4. What was Potiphar's job?

5. To whom is the book of Acts addressed?
    a) Theophilus
    b) Barnabas
    c) Cornelius
    d) Eutychus

1. What did Jesus do on a Sabbath day that so infuriated the Pharisees they began plotting to kill Him?

2. Where did Jesus move to after leaving Nazareth?
   a) Capernaum
   b) Jerusalem
   c) Cana
   d) Bethany

3. Who was Jesus' first disciple?

4. John says that to all who receive Jesus, to those who believe in His name, He gives the right to become _____ of God.

5. What name for Jesus, meaning "Anointed One," did Daniel use when writing about the end times?

1. What major prophet had a son named Shear-Jashub (NIV)?

2. When Gideon was visited by an angel, Gideon was hiding wheat from the
   a) Canaanites.
   b) Jebusites.
   c) Midianites.
   d) Electric Lights.

3. Whose wife was turned into a pillar of salt for looking back on the doomed cities of Sodom and Gomorrah?

4. Connect the Thots:
   son of Jephunneh
   associate of Joshua
   a positive report from Canaan

5. Match: Solomon. . .
   a) He asked God first for wealth and then for wisdom.
   b) He finished building the temple started by his father.
   c) His mother, Bathsheba, feared for her life before he was made king.

Answers:

1. Right after Jesus brought the little girl back to life, He healed
    a) a little boy who had only two fish and a loaf of
       bread for lunch.
    b) two blind men.
    c) three blind mice.
    d) ten lepers.

2. What violent act ended the reign of the evil king
   Zechariah of Israel only six months after he took power?

3. Connect the Thots:
    a six-month party
    a hanging
    a celebration called Purim

4. According to the apostle Paul, how will the day of Jesus'
   return come?
    a) like a thief in the night
    b) like a mighty trumpet
    c) like a flash of lightning
    d) like an eagle swooping

5. When told that his sons had been killed and the ark of
   the covenant had been taken, who fell over backward and
   died of a broken neck?

Answers:

5. Eli (1 Samuel 4:16–18)
4. a (1 Thessalonians 5:2)
3. events in the book of Esther (Esther 1:2–4; Esther 7:10; Esther 9:28)
2. assassination (2 Kings 15:8–10)
1. b (Matthew 9:24-29)

1. Complete the scripture:
   Thy word have I hid in mine heart, that I might not
   _____ against thee.

2. What does Romans 8:26 say that the Holy Spirit does
   for us?

3. According to Ecclesiastes, when should you "remember
   your Creator"?
   a) in the days of your youth
   b) when times of trouble come
   c) as your years increase
   d) in joy and in sorrow

4. What will the Counselor, who will live with you, teach
   you?

5. True or False: The God of Israel was not fooled by
   Jezebel's clever plan of revenge upon Naboth.

1. What businesswoman from Thyatira, a seller of purple cloth, became a Christian after hearing Paul share the Gospel?

2. Connect the Thots:
   Joanna the wife of Chuza
   Susanna
   Mary Magdalene

3. Match: Annas. . .
   a) blessed baby Jesus in the temple.
   b) was the father-in-law of Caiaphas.
   c) accompanied Paul on his second missionary journey.

4. In his letter to the Corinthians, who were the only people Paul said he baptized?

5. Who was promised that he would not die until he saw the Messiah come?

1. Where did Jesus pray the night He was betrayed and arrested?

2. Aaron died at
   a) Mount Sinai.
   b) the Mount of Olives.
   c) Mount Hor.
   d) Mount Everest.

3. What major body of water is less than twenty miles from Nazareth?

4. Match: Cush...
   a) Egypt
   b) Ethiopia
   c) Assyria

5. What did Abraham name the place where God told him to sacrifice Isaac?

Answers:

5. Jehovah-jireh: The Lord will provide (Genesis 22:1–14)

4. b (Isaiah 20, kjv/niv)

3. the Sea of Galilee

2. c (Numbers 33:38)

1. Gethsemane (Matthew 26:36–57)

1. Which of the following statements did Jesus make just before He died on the cross?
    a) "It is painful."
    b) "It is unfair."
    c) "It is finished."
    d) "It is necessary."

2. Where did Jesus say that a prophet is without honor?

3. Match: Jesus' sign for the Pharisees. . .
    a) sign of catastrophic weather
    b) sign of beheading of John the Baptist
    c) sign of Jonah

4. From what tribe did Jesus descend?

5. When a woman in Bethany poured expensive ointment on His head, Jesus
    a) said she had done something good for Him.
    b) was furious that his hairstyle was mussed.
    c) thought the gesture was a waste of money.
    d) sent her the bill for having His cloak dry cleaned.

Answers:

1. c (John 19:30 NIV)
2. in his hometown (Mark 6:4)
3. c (Matthew 16:1, 4 NIV)
4. Judah (Matthew 1:3–17 NIV)
5. a (Matthew 26:6–10)

1. What tiny insect did Jesus say the hypocritical Pharisees strained out of their food, only to "swallow a camel"?

2. Connect the Thots:
   beautiful on the mountains
   a sinful woman's kiss for Jesus
   God's Word as a lamp

3. What did the four living creatures around the throne resemble, respectively?

4. How many golden lampstands, each representing a church in Asia Minor, did John see in his vision of the Revelation of Christ?
   a) three
   b) five
   c) seven
   d) nine

5. What body fluid did God forbid the Israelites to eat because it holds the life of every creature?

1. What idol were the Israelites worshipping with shouting and singing when Moses arrived with God's Ten Commandments?

2. Connect the Thots:
   adulterers
   extortioners
   drunkards

3. What grew from the ground God cursed after Adam and Eve's sin?

4. What was Jesus' command to the members of the church at Ephesus, who had "left thy first love"?
   a) weep
   b) repent
   c) pray
   d) yearn

5. Who is the man, Jesus says, who does not enter the sheep pen by the gate but climbs in some other way?

1. How did Paul describe everything he had lost in his life in his efforts to gain Christ?

2. The Epistle of James tells Christians how to
   a) set up the Communion table.
   b) write a proper thank-you note.
   c) write a Sunday school curriculum for toddlers.
   d) live according to God's Word.

3. Jesus said, "The Spirit gives life," but what "counts for nothing"?

4. Complete the scripture:
   He lifted up himself, and said unto them, He that is without sin among you, let him first cast a _____ at her.

5. Whom did the five foolish virgins ask for oil for their lamps?

Answers:

5. the five wise virgins (Matthew 25:1, 8)
4. stone (John 8:7 KJV)
3. the flesh (John 6:63 NIV)
2. d
1. rubbish, or dung (Philippians 3:7–8)

Quiz
230

1. What did Samson eat from the carcass of a lion he had killed?

2. Connect the Thots:
   Absalom
   Samson
   Mary, sister of Martha

3. What part of the body is usually anointed?

4. Match: Lot...
   a) baked bread without yeast for two angels.
   b) refused to eat bread before Sodom was destroyed.
   c) baked bread to take with him out of Sodom.

5. What job was Moses doing when God spoke to him from the burning bush?

Answers:

1. honey (Judges 14:5–9)
2. people famed for their hair (2 Samuel 14:25–26; Judges 16:13–17; John 11:1–2)
3. the head (1 Samuel 10:1)
4. a (Genesis 19:1, 3)
5. herding sheep (Exodus 3:1–2)

1. With what does Psalm 45 say that Jesus has been anointed?

2. Connect the Thots:
   the first and the last
   the light of the world
   the way, the truth, and the life

3. According to Paul, from what curse has Christ redeemed us?

4. Complete the scripture:
   Who shall _____ us from the love of Christ? shall tribulation, or distress, or persecution, or famine, or nakedness, or peril, or sword?

5. Speaking of the future, Jesus tells of wars, earthquakes, and famines that are to come. By standing firm, He says, we will gain _____.

● ● ● ● ● ● ● ● ● ● ●

1. What prophetess told the faithful King Josiah he would not see the disaster God was bringing on his unfaithful nation?

2. Jezebel killed Naboth so Ahab could possess his
   a) slaves.
   b) flocks.
   c) gold.
   d) vineyard.

3. What Old Testament priest, for whom a Bible book is named, worked with Nehemiah to encourage the public reading and study of scripture?

4. Connect the Thots:
   Don't drink wine.
   Don't cut your hair.
   Don't touch the dead.

5. Match: Hezekiah. . .
   a) He was the last king of Israel.
   b) As a sign to him, God made the shadow go forward ten steps on a sundial.
   c) God added fifteen years to his life.

Answers:

5. c (2 Kings 20:1, 6)
4. rules for the Nazarite vow (Numbers 6:1–8)
3. Ezra (Nehemiah 8:1–12)
2. d (1 Kings 21:5–15)
1. Huldah (2 Kings 22:3, 14–20)

1. What annual celebration was instituted to commemorate the Jews' victory over their enemies in Queen Esther's time?

2. When Mary Magdalene first saw the risen Christ, she believed He was
   a) an angel.
   b) the gardener.
   c) a disciple playing a prank.
   d) John the Baptist.

3. Connect the Thots:
   the earth quakes and rocks split
   graves open and the bodies of saints come back to life
   the veil of the temple tears from top to bottom

4. What did Jesus tell the servants in Cana to do with the six stone water jars?

5. Which of the following was not one of Satan's temptations of Christ?
   a) changing stones into bread
   b) jumping off the temple
   c) worshiping the devil
   d) striking the wicked with blindness

Answers:

5. d (Matthew 4:1–10)
4. fill them with water (John 2:7)
3. Jesus' death (Matthew 27:50–53)
2. b (John 20:1, 15)
1. Purim (Esther 9:20–28)

1. The apostle Paul warned Christians about being "yoked" with what?
   a) debt
   b) unbelievers
   c) sin
   d) worldly wisdom

2. Complete the scripture:
   All scripture is given by _____ of God, and is profitable for doctrine, for reproof, for correction, for instruction in righteousness.

3. According to Acts 8:39, what did the Holy Spirit do with Philip?

4. Which of the following is not on the apostle Paul's list of things to think about?
   a) whatever is true
   b) whatever is pure
   c) whatever is lovely
   d) whatever is pleasing

5. "Peace I leave with you; my peace I give you." To what peace was Jesus referring?

Answers:

5. the peace conveyed by the Holy Spirit (John 14:27 niv)

4. d (Philippians 4:8)

3. caught him away

2. inspiration (2 Timothy 3:16 kjv)

1. b (2 Corinthians 6:14)

1. What wandering preacher was imprisoned for challenging the adulterous marriage of King Herod?

2. Which of the following is *not* a hardship the apostle Paul had to endure, according to his list in 2 Corinthians 11?
    a) shipwreck
    b) beatings
    c) wild animals
    d) robbers

3. What was Matthew's job before he became a disciple of Jesus?

4. Connect the Thots:
    Tabitha
    helping the poor
    death and resurrection

5. True or False: When Jesus told Martha that Lazarus would rise again, she thought He meant Lazarus would rise again at the resurrection at the last day.

Answers:

1. John the Baptist (Mark 6:14–18)
2. c (2 Corinthians 11:23–28)
3. tax collector (Matthew 9:9)
4. Dorcas (Acts 9:36–41)
5. True (John 11:23–24)

Quiz
236

• • • • • • • • • • • •

1. What land did the patriarch Abraham hail from?

2. Connect the Thots:
   Carmel
   Hermon
   Zion

3. In what city did Jesus' disciples first take the name "Christians"?

4. Match: Valley of Rephaim. . .
   a) where Abner was murdered
   b) where David twice attacked the Philistines
   c) where Saul died after battling the Philistines

5. What did Moses fear the thirsty Israelites would do to him at a dry place called Rephidim?

Answers:

5. stone him (Exodus 17:1–4)
4. b (2 Samuel 5:17–25)
3. Antioch (Acts 11:26)
2. mountains (1 Kings 18:19; Deuteronomy 3:8; Psalm 74:2)
1. Ur of the Chaldees, or Chaldeans (Genesis 15:1, 7–8)

1. Why did Pilate's wife advise her husband to leave Jesus alone?
    a) She believed Isaiah's prophecies.
    b) She had seen Jesus perform miracles.
    c) She had had a bad dream.
    d) She feared a Galilean revolt.

2. As Jesus rode the donkey toward Jerusalem, what did the people throw down on the road?

3. Which of the following was not a gift the wise men brought the baby Jesus?
    a) gold
    b) diamonds
    c) frankincense
    d) myrrh

4. According to the Gospel of Mark, what did evil spirits do whenever they saw Jesus, and what did they say?

5. Match: Powers Jesus gave the disciples. . .
    a) to drive out demons and restore sight.
    b) to drive out demons and heal all diseases.
    c) to heal all diseases.

Answers:

1. What stinging insect did God use to drive enemy peoples out of the Promised Land?

2. Connect the Thots:
   Pharaoh's lost in the Red Sea
   Solomon's 1,400
   Elijah's fiery ride into heaven

3. What melting substance did the psalmist say his heart had turned to?

4. What precious metal, according to Proverbs, cannot compare to the value of wisdom?
   a) silver
   b) bronze
   c) gold
   d) iron

5. What was the sacrifice that Joseph and Mary were required to offer up for Jesus' birth?

Answers:

5. two turtledoves or two young pigeons (Luke 2:21–24)

4. c (Proverbs 16:16)

3. wax (Psalm 22:14)

2. chariots (Exodus 14:28; 2 Chronicles 1:14; 2 Kings 2:11)

1. hornet (Joshua 24:11–12)

1. Connect the thots:
   fig leaves
   a curse
   dust

2. Complete the scripture:
   For if you _____ men when they sin against you, your
   heavenly Father will also _____ you.

3. What do the Proverbs call the person who tries to add to
   God's Words?
   a) a liar
   b) a fool
   c) a cheat
   d) a devil

4. Who was Korah, and what happened to him?

5. Match: Jacob...
   a) wore Esau's best clothes with goatskin on his arms
      and neck.
   b) wore Esau's poorest garments with goatskin on his
      arms and neck.
   c) wore his own clothes and goatskin on his arms and
      neck.

Answers:

5. a (Genesis 27:15–16)
4. He led a rebellion against Moses and Aaron and was swallowed by the
   earth (Numbers 16).
3. a (Proverbs 30:6)
2. forgive, forgive (Matthew 6:14 NIV)
1. the sin of Adam and Eve (Genesis 3:7; Genesis 3:17; Genesis 3:19)

1. What answer did Jesus give to an expert in the law who asked which commandment was greatest?

2. Complete the scripture:
   The effectual fervent prayer of a _____ man availeth much.

3. How did Jesus say you could recognize a tree?

4. 1 Peter was written to help
   a) raise money for new carpet in the sanctuary.
   b) Christians find other Christian businesses.
   c) suffering Christians.
   d) missionaries in South America.

5. What did the merchant do when he found the pearl of great price?

Answers:

1. "Love the Lord your God with all your heart and with all your soul and with all your mind" (Matthew 22:34–40 NIV).
2. righteous (James 5:16 KJV)
3. by its fruit (Matthew 12:33)
4. c
5. sold all he had and bought it (Matthew 13:45–46)

1. Which of the following does not appear in Song of Solomon?
   a) "Your nose is like the tower of Lebanon."
   b) "Your navel is a rounded goblet."
   c) "Your fingers are like limbs of cedar."
   d) "Your eyes are the pools of Heshbon."

2. What gruesome things did Ezekiel see filling a valley?

3. Connect the Thots:
   Abimelech's injury
   Jezebel's remains
   Golgotha

4. Match: Seventeen. . .
   a) years Samson was judge of Israel
   b) shekels of silver paid to Judas for his betrayal
   c) shekels of silver paid by Jeremiah for a field

5. Which famous Bible character shared his name with a lesser-known biblical woman?
   a) Adam
   b) Daniel
   c) Moses
   d) Noah

Answers:

1. c (Song of Solomon 7:1–5 NIV)
2. dry bones (Ezekiel 37:1–14)
3. skulls (Judges 9:52–53; 2 Kings 9:34–37; Mark 15:22)
4. c (Jeremiah 32:9)
5. d (Numbers 27:1)

1. When many followers decided to leave Jesus because of His controversial teachings, how many of the twelve disciples left?

2. Connect the Thots:
   a slave and an awl
   false teachers and things that itch
   Peter and Malchus

3. Match: Jesus' clearing of the temple...
   a) once
   b) twice
   c) three times

4. What does John 3:17 say that God did not send Jesus to do?

5. Which of the following is not among the names of Christ in Isaiah's prophecy?
   a) Mighty God
   b) Everlasting Father
   c) Prince of Peace
   d) Hope of Man

1. What handsome son of Jacob was imprisoned after a false report from Potiphar's wife?

2. Connect the Thots:
   Eliphaz
   Zophar
   Elihu

3. What man, cousin of Queen Esther, served as her adviser and saved the Jews from destruction?

4. Connect the Thots:
   son of Saul
   warrior of Israel
   friend of David

5. Match: Jeroboam. . .
   a) He was told by a prophet that he would rule ten tribes in Israel.
   b) Solomon chose him as his successor.
   c) He built his own shrines at Jerusalem.

Answers:

5. a (1 Kings 11:29–31)
4. Jonathan (1 Samuel 14:1; 1 Samuel 14:14; 1 Samuel 20:42)
3. Mordecai (Esther 2:7; 10:3)
2. characters in the book of Job (Job 4:1; Job 20:1; Job 32:2)
1. Joseph (Genesis 39:2–20)

1. Who was to die in Egyptian households on the night of Passover?

2. Elijah, a man of God, was taken to heaven
   a) in a whirlwind.
   b) in a chariot.
   c) up a stairway.
   d) by climbing a ladder.

3. What miraculous event preceded Jesus walking on water toward His disciples?

4. Connect the Thots:
   Stephen is stoned to death.
   Saul is converted to faith in Jesus.
   An angel releases Peter from prison.

5. What, according to 1 Corinthians, will be "swallowed up in victory" at the last trumpet?

1. How long does the psalmist say that a thousand years are in God's sight?

2. Complete the scripture:
   Prophecy came not in old time by the _____ of man: but holy men of God spake as they were moved by the Holy Ghost.

3. What three things did Paul tell Timothy that God has given us, as opposed to a spirit of fear?

4. What type of people, according to the book of James, does God give grace to?
   a) the wise
   b) the merciful
   c) the peacemakers
   d) the humble

5. What parable illustrates how God feels about those who don't forgive others?

1. What woman, also known as Tabitha, was raised from the dead after Peter knelt and prayed?

2. Connect the Thots:
   Aceldama
   a kiss
   thirty pieces of silver

3. Match: Mary. . .
   a) sang to Elizabeth after her baby leaped in her womb.
   b) sang to Joseph after her baby leaped in her womb.
   c) sang to the angel Gabriel.

4. True or False: According to Peter, you can trust any person who claims to be a Christian.

5. After the crucifixion, who asked Pilate for Jesus' body?
   a) Simon of Cyrene
   b) Joseph of Arimathea
   c) Mary of Magdala
   d) Apollos of Alexandria

Answers:

5. b (Mark 15:43)
4. False (2 Peter 2:1)
3. a (Luke 1:39–55)
2. Judas Iscariot (Acts 1:16–19 kjv; Luke 22:47–48; Matthew 27:3–4)
1. Dorcas (Acts 9:36–41)

1. What mount saw the deaths of King Saul and his sons in battle?

2. Match: Garden of Eden...
   a) where Adam and Eve ate from the tree of life
   b) where Adam and Eve ate from the tree of knowledge of good and evil
   c) where the tree of life was not found

3. The leaves of the tree of life in the new heaven on earth will be used for what purpose?

4. Where did Lot, apparently unwilling to move too far from the soon-to-be-destroyed Sodom, beg God's angels to let him live?
   a) Gaza
   b) Haran
   c) Ur
   d) Zoar

5. What was special about the Pool of Bethesda?

Answers:

5. an angel stirred up the water, and the first one in after that would be healed (John 5:2–4 kjv)

4. d (Genesis 19:1–22)

3. the healing of nations (Revelation 22:2)

2. b (Genesis 2:15–16, 3:17)

1. Gilboa (1 Samuel 31:8)

Quiz
248

1. What was Jesus discussing when He mentioned the name of Caesar?
    a) the fall of Rome
    b) idolatry
    c) paying taxes
    d) unjust leadership

2. Complete the scripture:
For God did not send his Son into the world to condemn the world, but to _____ the world through him.

3. Match: Anointing of Jesus. . .
    a) done by Martha, Lazarus's sister
    b) done by pouring perfume on His head
    c) done at the home of Lazarus in Bethany

4. What did the risen Jesus say to Mary Magdalene?

5. How many apostles did Jesus personally select?
    a) two
    b) twelve
    c) fifty
    d) one thousand

Answers:

5. b (Luke 6:13)
4. "Why are you crying?" (John 20:11–15 NIV)
3. b (Mark 14:1–3)
2. save (John 3:17 NIV)
1. c (Luke 20:21–25)

1. What valuable red stones, according to Proverbs, are worth less than either wisdom or a good wife?

2. Connect the Thots:
   the earth, to God
   enemies, to Christ
   a place of dishonor, to the poor

3. What food was to be stored in the ark of the covenant?

4. What sign protected Israelite homes in Egypt from the plague on the firstborn?
   a) a candle in the window
   b) bread in the oven
   c) a goat in the yard
   d) blood on the doorposts

5. What beast of burden was forbidden as food to the Israelites?

Answers:

1. rubies (Proverbs 8:11; 31:10)
2. footstools (Isaiah 66:1; Matthew 22:41–45; James 2:3)
3. pot of manna (Exodus 16:32–34)
4. d (Exodus 12:23)
5. camel (Leviticus 11:4)

Quiz
250